CARDIOVASCULAR
TRAINING
FOR FITNESS

CARDIOVASCULAR
TRAINING
FOR FITNESS

**STEP-BY-STEP FITNESS CONDITIONING FROM WARM-UPS
TO WORKOUTS, SHOWN IN 390 PHOTOGRAPHS**

**PRACTICAL TRAINING PLANS FOR LOSING WEIGHT,
GAINING MUSCLE, TONING UP, SWIMMING,
SIX-PACK AND TRIATHLON**

ANDY WADSWORTH

HERMES
HOUSE

This edition is published by Hermes House,
an imprint of Anness Publishing Ltd, Blaby Road,
Wigston, Leicestershire LE18 4SE

Email: info@anness.com

Web: www.hermeshouse.com; www.annesspublishing.com

If you like the images in this book and would like to investigate
using them for publishing, promotions or advertising, please visit our
website www.practicalpictures.com for more information.

Publisher: Joanna Lorenz
Project Editor: Anne Hildyard
Designer: Nigel Partridge
Illustrator: Peter Bull
Proofreading Manager: Lindsay Zamponi
Production Controller: Christine Ni

Previously published as part of a larger volume, *The Illustrated
Practical Encyclopedia of Fitness Training*

ETHICAL TRADING POLICY
At Anness Publishing we believe that business should be conducted
in an ethical and ecologically sustainable way, with respect for
the environment and a proper regard to the replacement of the
natural resources we employ. As a publisher, we use a lot of wood
pulp to make high-quality paper for printing, and that wood
commonly comes from spruce trees. We are therefore currently
growing more than 750,000 trees in three Scottish forest
plantations: Berrymoss (130 hectares/320 acres), West Touxhill
(125 hectares/305 acres) and Deveron Forest (75 hectares/
185 acres). The forests we manage contain more than 3.5 times
the number of trees employed each year in making paper for
the books we manufacture. Because of this ongoing ecological
investment programme, you, as our customer, can have the pleasure
and reassurance of knowing that a tree is being cultivated on
your behalf to naturally replace the materials used to make the
book you are holding.
Our forestry programme is run in accordance with the UK
Woodland Assurance Scheme (UKWAS) and will be certified by the
internationally recognized Forest Stewardship Council (FSC).
The FSC is a non-government organization dedicated
to promoting responsible management of the world's forests.
Certification ensures forests are managed in an environmentally
sustainable and socially responsible way. For further information
about this scheme, go to www.annesspublishing.com/trees

PUBLISHER'S NOTE
Although the advice and information in this book are believed
to be accurate and true at the time of going to press, neither
the authors nor the publisher can accept any legal responsibility
or liability for any errors or omissions that may be made nor
for any inaccuracies nor for any loss, harm or injury that comes
about from following instructions or advice in this book.

CONTENTS

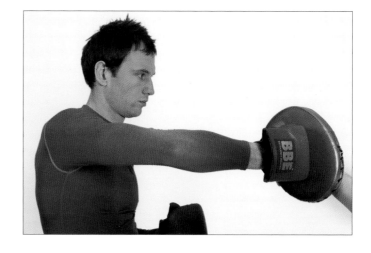

Introduction to Exercise

Going to the gym and jumping on the treadmill will not necessarily give you the results you want from your exercise regime. There are so many different exercises that you can do, some of them far more beneficial than others.

This book will give you an understanding of which exercises will help you to achieve your goals, with detailed descriptions of how and when to do them so that you can be confident that you are exercising correctly. To achieve fast, effective, long-lasting results you will need variation in your training. Each exercise lists the muscles used so you can determine which part of your body is being exercised, giving you the chance to change your exercises and challenge your body to promote better results.

This is a chance to create the new you – a healthy mind and a fit body. You will grow in confidence as you learn more about yourself, how to test your fitness, and which exercises work for you.

Before you begin exercising, decide what you want from your exercise routine. Do you want a six-pack for a summer beach holiday? Is building muscle or losing weight important for you? Whether it is looking great for your wedding day or staying fit through pregnancy, de-stressing or keeping fit while travelling, beating the opposition on the sports field or trying to stay young that interests you, there is a plan for achieving your goal in this book.

It's not just exercise that will make you fit and healthy; nutrition is just as important. Everything you eat has some effect on you – your food can turn to fat or energize you; it can help you to improve your fitness level, recover from exercise, change your body shape and alter your self-image. This book will provide you with an understanding of the effect that different foods have, the optimum nutrition combination and the best time to eat and drink.

There is always some exercise you can do. Even if you are injured, there are exercises that will help you to recover. This book provides you with basic knowledge to help with diagnosing injury, understanding the recovery process and preventing the injury from recurring.

Exercise is not just about sweating buckets in the gym. Core stability and flexibility training are just as important to prevent injury and give you the strength to train harder, push big weights, run marathons or cope with the demands of everyday life.

Regular exercising will not only help you to gain physical fitness, providing a big boost to your self-esteem; you will also have increased energy, and benefit from a more active and positive outlook.

Right: There are no short cuts to getting fit, but it is much easier if you have the right information about appropriate training.

GETTING STARTED

Before you begin your journey to a fitter lifestyle, this chapter outlines a realistic approach to a successful fitness training programme, including accurately assessing your starting point, setting achievable goals, taking and analysing body measurements, performing fitness tests to measure your progress, keeping a training diary, and determining which exercises are best for you. Armed with this new knowledge, you will come to appreciate why you are not intended to live a sedentary lifestyle, and commit to making health and exercise priorities in your life.

Above: Whatever your fitness goals may be, you will certainly enjoy achieving them.
Left: Fitness training will help you discover more about yourself.

Three Steps to Fitness

We are bombarded today, on one hand, by news items stressing the importance of a healthy lifestyle, and on the other by pictures of glamorous celebrities. Can you ever look that good? Yes, but not by wishing for it – it takes determination, motivation and knowledge.

As everyone knows – or should – there is no such thing as overnight success in any walk of life, and certainly not in the area of health and fitness. Unfortunately, we live in a culture of conflicting messages that do nothing to nourish our wellbeing. On the one hand, it is impossible to escape media images of thin, toned, buffed and sculpted role models of quite out-of-reach physical perfection. On the other, advertising and the food industry pump fat-filled, sugar-coated, carbohydrate-rich food at us from every direction. Consequently, we

Below: Hours of training steps up all the systems in your body and helps you to run faster.

Above: You don't need to be in the gym for this type of floor exercise; you can easily do it at home.

Above: The buzz you get from being supremely fit will help you continue your fitness regime.

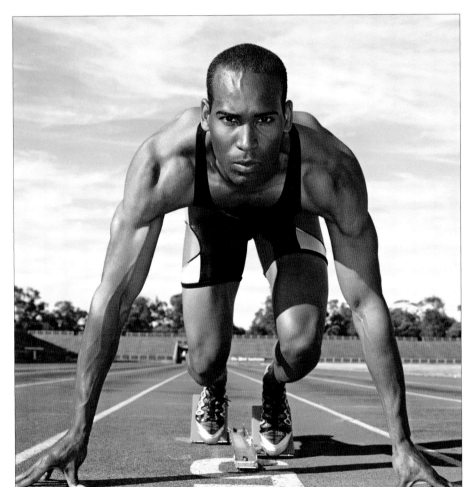

have become an unfit society in thrall to endless aspiration, and sold on the promise of nips, tucks, jabs, instant gratification and quick fixes. Quite simply, becoming fit and healthy – safely, effectively and in the long term – does not and will not happen quickly. You will, however, get real results if you follow this three-step plan:

Determination Look at other areas of your life in which determination has been a force for change, such as passing exams, bringing up your children in the best way possible, getting a better job or making more money. Transfer some of this determination to the job of making yourself fit and healthy.

Motivation Have a goal in mind, such as running a half-marathon, fitting into a wedding dress or simply getting up the stairs without being out of breath.

Fitness can't be bought
Simply paying a monthly subscription to a gym is not enough to help you get fitter. You can buy many things in life, but fitness involves regular, hard work.

Correct training

Watching people exercising in the gym and copying them is not the way to get the best results, because many people cheat to make the exercise easier.

Use this chapter to determine your goals by analysing all aspects of your life and making a note of your strengths and weaknesses. Once you have set your goals, keep visualizing how great you will feel once you have achieved them. This is something you are doing for yourself and no one else. Family and friends can try to motivate you but until you actually want to do it for yourself, it won't work. After all, no one is asking them to make sacrifices – you are the one who has to change your lifestyle and do the physical training.

Knowledge Gather as much knowledge as possible to plan your new personal training plan. It is not possible to get results without understanding how your

Below: If you want to succeed in your aims quickly, get help and advice from professionals in the field.

body works and what type of training will be best for you. Be aware, though, that a little knowledge can be a bad thing. For example, the suggestion that resistance training will make you gain weight is a myth. The truth is that resistance training will make you gain lean muscle mass, which will have a positive effect on your metabolism and therefore make you lose fat.

Knowing what to eat, and when to eat it, is also essential. Without good nutrition, you won't have the energy to train, recover from training or see the benefits of your training. There are no short cuts or quick fixes – your nutrition plan will require preparation to make it practical for you to stick with it every day.

Know yourself

Once you have the basic knowledge, you can apply the correct training to achieve your goals. In some ways you have far more knowledge of yourself than a gym instructor because they have only known you for a matter of hours, whereas you have known yourself since the day you were born. You know how determined you can be and what your motivation is. You know what you enjoy and what you dislike. You can be honest with yourself about how you look and

Above: Just a little extra fitness can mean the difference between winning and losing.

how you want to look. You know how much energy you have and how much more energy you would like to have. Your exercise plan has to suit you and no one else.

Plan ahead

Be practical and think ahead. For example, if you are travelling for business or on holiday, plan your training to be harder in the week before and after you are away. Don't use the time away as an excuse – there is always some kind of training you can do, whether it's going for a run or doing exercises in your hotel room. Keep your goal in sight and remember that consistency is the key to achieving it.

No excuses

There are two types of people who want to get fit: those who think about results and those who think of excuses. If you look for excuses, you are setting yourself up to fail. If you focus on achieving results, you will win. From the moment you pick up this book, the excuses stop and you set yourself on the path to success – to fitness and health.

A Lifestyle that Works for Your Body

One of the main reasons for a general lack of fitness in developed societies is that so many people lead sedentary lifestyles, and abuse their bodies daily through poor diet and other bad habits. The simple fact is – we are not designed for the way we live.

Compare your lifestyle with that of someone who lived approximately 10,000 years ago. When people lived as hunter-gatherers, constantly on the move looking for food, they led very active lives.

From hunter-gatherers to channel-flickers

Today, many people lead an unhealthy desk-bound, sofa-lounging, channel-flicking lifestyle, their longest walk being to the car and back. It's time to take stock of the fact that although we live in post-industrial, urban environments, our bodies have not evolved to keep pace with the demands of life in this developed world. We are still built to live as our ancestors did, many thousands of years ago. Unfortunately, that's causing us a lot of problems. Take control of your lifestyle before it's too late.

Below: If children are encouraged to try a sport when they are young, it will stand them in good stead later on.

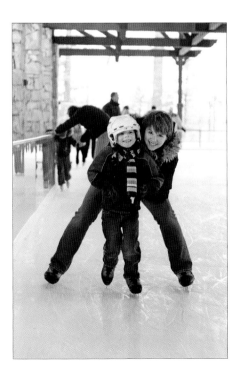

Life expectancy and lifestyle

There is a direct correlation between life expectancy and lifestyle. A person who drinks excessive amounts of alcohol, smokes, eats unhealthily and lives a sedentary lifestyle will have a shorter life expectancy than someone who looks after their body and takes regular exercise. However, it is not just about the length of your life. Quality of life is just as important, and if you don't take care of yourself, your life will not only be shorter, it may well be unpleasant too.

Most disturbing of all, there is ample evidence that these bad habits are starting earlier and earlier in life. Little to no exercise or outdoor games, endless hours sitting in front of computer games and a diet high in sugar and saturated fat have triggered escalating and alarming rates of obesity and related illnesses among children. The net result will be, if left unchecked, a generation of children likely to live shorter lives than their parents.

Above: Children thrive on fresh air and exercise; limit the time spent playing computer games indoors.

Our healthy ancestors

We know people lived relatively healthily 10,000 years ago because there are people still living the same lifestyle in some areas of the world today – the last 84 tribes of hunter-gatherers in the world, who can be found in Australia, Africa and South America. Fit with lean muscular physiques, these people continue to live very active and healthy lives, and experience markedly lower levels of diseases such as cancer and heart disease.

This much we know

People in the developed world cannot go back in time, but they can get an understanding of what they should do to find a balance in their lifestyle, in order to stay healthy. We know that exercise makes you fitter, boosting your immune system and protecting you from

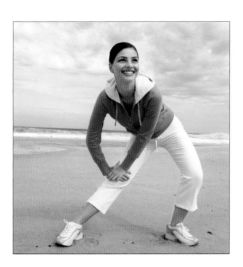

Above: Sea air and exercise is a great combination for a healthy and happy way of life.

disease. We know that some exercise each day will counteract the negative effects of sitting at a desk all day staring at a computer screen, and will give you the get-up-and-go to have fun with family and friends. We know that eating certain foods will give you energy and make you look good and feel good. Let's take this knowledge and put it to good use so that we can all live longer and happier lives.

Below: Your body is not designed to sit in a car all day. Try to change your mode of transport to include walking.

The perils of modern-day life

There are many aspects of modern life that are intrinsically bad for our physical and mental wellbeing. From the daily grind of office life to the stresses and strains of travel and the junk food that we consume, living in a developed country has a downside.

Desk-bound injuries Sitting still in front of a computer all day long, and doing no exercise, contributes to back and neck problems. Physiotherapists and osteopaths owe most of their income to this fact. Correct exercise would prevent all of these problems – problems that didn't exist generations ago. We didn't need core-stability exercises to avoid such aches and pains, because working the land made these muscles strong.

Mental exhaustion We are not designed to work long hours and feel stressed about hitting deadlines. The body is designed to hunt and gather, then rest and build strength for the next day. Having to retain huge amounts of information can be exhausting; it leaves you feeling too mentally tired to do any exercise. Of course, taking exercise will provide you with the energy to continue to hit targets and deadlines at work, and enable you to work long hours.

Travel woes We were not intended to travel in planes or for any great length of time by other means of transport.

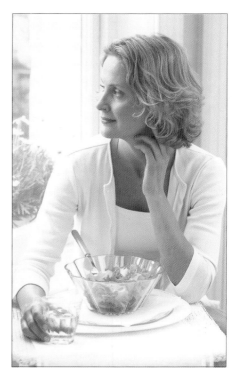

Above: Fast food is fine occasionally, but it is good to be aware of your body's nutritional needs and eat healthily.

Travelling through time zones, especially at altitude in a short space of time, can be very tiring, and of course there are the additional negative effects of sitting still for hours.

Junk food and booze We are not designed to eat convenience foods, which are often full of sugar that will affect your energy levels and body weight. Alcohol is viewed as a natural accompaniment to food, but even modest amounts of alcohol can lead to a number of illnesses and damage to some of the major organs of the body. Even if food is 'natural', the nutritional content may only be a fraction of what it was many years ago. In many areas, the land has been over-farmed and saturated with chemicals, which leaves crops tainted with an unhealthy chemical residue.

Labour-saving, life-shortening We were not designed to use labour-saving devices. We were designed to use our hands and the materials from the land to build shelters and weapons to catch animals and provide food. Today, there is a gadget or machine for almost everything, which simply encourages us to become lazier still.

The Importance of Exercise

Regular exercise leaves you full of vitality and a get-up-and-go attitude. People who do physical training regularly already know that if they skip a few days they start to feel tired and lethargic, which is how many people feel who never exercise.

The right exercise and nutrition can dramatically reduce the risk of many common illnesses and diseases, including cardiovascular disease, various cancers and type II diabetes:

Heart disease Exercising three to four times a week and eating healthily have a positive effect on your heart. Exercise also lowers cholesterol levels and blood pressure, which considerably reduces the chances of suffering a heart attack.

Osteoporosis Regular weight-bearing exercise helps to build bone tissue and prevent age-related bone-density loss.

Cancer Exercise reduces the risk of some cancers. Two ovarian hormones that are linked to breast cancer, estradiol and progesterone, are reduced by exercise. Studies have shown that regular exercise can help prevent breast cancer by up to 60 per cent. Several studies also show that obese people who live sedentary lives are at increased risk of endometrial, colon, gall bladder, prostate and kidney cancers.

Below: If you attempt to practise a healthy lifestyle, you are less likely to worry about the doctor's findings.

Above: Sporting injuries should always be assessed by a professional.

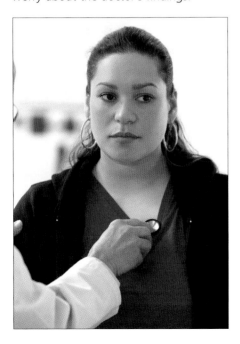

Type II diabetes Regular exercise will dramatically reduce the risk of developing type II diabetes. A weight increase of 5–10kg/11–22lb doubles the risk of developing type II diabetes. More than 80 per cent of people with type II diabetes are overweight or obese, which is why it is also referred to sometimes as 'diabesity'.

Joint and back pain These common ailments can be reduced with the correct physical training, which will build muscle and increase flexibility and core stability.

Obesity A combination of cardiovascular and strength training will increase the metabolism and improve the body's capacity to burn calories. This helps to

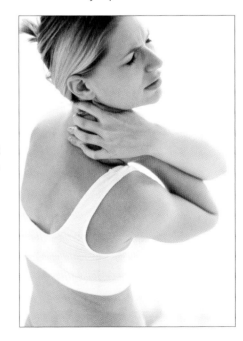

Right: Regular physical exercise can greatly reduce unpleasant neck pain and headaches.

reduce the risk of developing one of the many obesity-related diseases as well as increasing wellbeing.

Psychological health The symptoms of depression and anxiety can be reduced by regular exercise. Stress is part of everyday life but exercise can equip you to cope with it. Exercise will give you greater endurance to tackle daily tasks, improve your sleep, increase your energy and give you an improved body shape, which will improve your self-esteem.

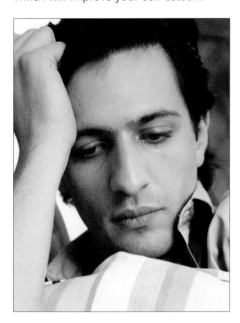

Above: Lack of exercise can have the effect of making you feel lethargic and demotivated.

Below: Fruits are a healthy alternative to sugary or fatty snacks.

General health Regular exercise has many health benefits. It can boost some vital processes in the body, such as stimulating your digestion, liver function and your glycogen system (stored glucose, mainly in the muscles and the liver). Exercise will lead to an improved immune system, it can revitalize and enhance your sex life, and may well add some years to your life. Strength training has the ability to tone, build and improve the speed of muscle contraction and reaction time through the development of strong neuromuscular pathways. You will also become more agile and benefit in many ways from improved co-ordination and balance.

Don't put it off
Fear is one of the biggest factors in motivating exercise. If you were to stand in a line of 100 people waiting for a heart attack, where in the queue would you be? If you are near the front, then fear will probably be the motivating factor that drives you to a healthier lifestyle, but why should it be this way? Be healthy before you get to the fear stage. Most importantly, respect your body – it's the only one you've got – and aim to feel good on the inside and the outside by exercising regularly.

Below: Regular strength, flexibility and core-stability training can help to prevent back pain.

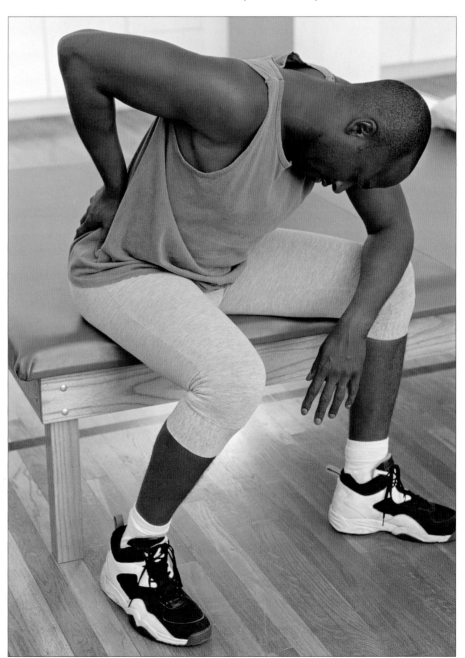

Setting Your Goals

Before you start to exercise, you must be clear about what it is you want to achieve. Do you want to run a marathon, lose weight or gain muscle? These are all big goals and in order to achieve them, you need to prepare both your body and your mind.

Begin by setting out smaller goals. For example, if you want to run a marathon in six months' time, set yourself deadlines, such as being able to run 10km/6.2 miles after the first two months of training, and 20km/12.4 miles after three months. A gradual improvement in stamina and ability will help you to focus on the big goal.

There are also other factors to take into consideration, such as what it will be like to run among so many other athletes. Research the marathon course and talk to people who have run it previously so that you are familiar with its organization and structure. Consider the equipment you intend to use, your fluid intake and tactics for the big event. Running a half-marathon is an excellent way to get first-hand marathon experience. Plan when to change your training shoes in order to get the best

out of them, but do not turn up on the start line with shoes that are worn out or brand new shoes that may give you injuries or blisters. Read around the subject of injury so that you can identify early signs of injury immediately.

If you want to lose weight, follow a six-week plan that incorporates a low GI diet and exercise. So that you can monitor your weight loss and progress, keep a training diary.

When you want to gain muscle, plan your training sessions carefully, enlisting the help of a personal trainer if necessary. They will be able to help with the appropriate type of exercises for specific muscles.

Make your own goal wheel

It is important to focus on other factors in your life that will have an effect on your goal. For example, if you want to

Above: Even if you don't succeed immediately, there is nothing wrong with setting long-term goals.

lose weight, you will struggle if you have low self-esteem, suffer from lack of sleep and work too hard to do any exercise. Use a goal wheel to help you change your lifestyle and keep achieving. The goal wheel is similar to the wheel of a bicycle. The wheel has an outer rim, a hub in the centre and spokes running between the rim and the hub. Each of these spokes represents a different factor in your life. Because people's lives are very different, you can make the spokes represent whatever you like.

An example would be spokes for physical exercise, social life, nutrition, sleep, family, work, injury and psychology. Each spoke has a score

Timeline

Whatever your goal, set yourself a timeline, starting with where you are now and ending with where you want to get to. Place your smaller goals on the timeline and add notes next to the timeline reminding you of the other factors that will help you to achieve your goal, such as good nutrition.

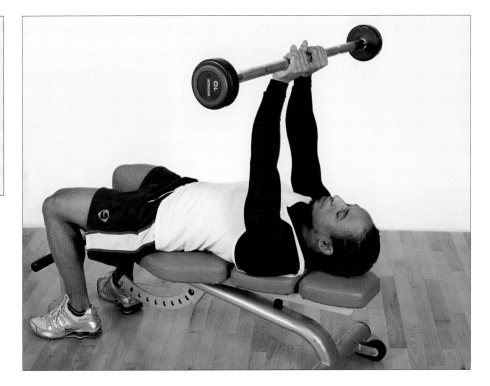

on it going from ten at the hub to zero at the rim. You personalize your wheel by putting a cross on each spoke. For example, if you take little or no physical exercise, you would put a cross close to the rim of the physical exercise spoke. If your exercise routine is going well and you really enjoy it, mark a cross close to the hub.

Once you have put a cross on each spoke, join the crosses up. It is highly likely that you will have a jagged pattern within the wheel. Some crosses will be close to the hub and others will be farther away. Every spoke that has a cross close to the rim of the wheel represents the lifestyle factor that you need to work on. It is important to

remember that all the factors are related. For example, your psychology score may be low if you never take any exercise and your nutrition is poor. If you spend all your time working and socializing and especially if this involves a lot of drinking alcohol, you won't be able to run a marathon successfully.

Above: Always keep in mind the goals you have set yourself; this should help you stick to the training.

There simply won't be enough time to train adequately, and if you try to take part, it could result in feelings of depression and even physical injury.

Below: Getting weighed weekly will help you assess the progress you are making in your training plan.

Goal wheel

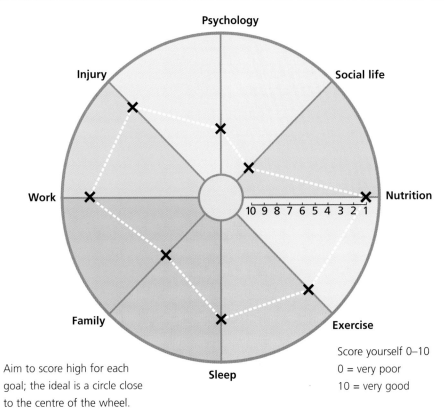

Aim to score high for each goal; the ideal is a circle close to the centre of the wheel.

Score yourself 0–10
0 = very poor
10 = very good

Training Diary

Keeping a training diary will help you to achieve your goals and stay motivated. Make the diary realistic and useful. Don't cram it with information that will become irrelevant later on in training – only note facts that motivate you and help you to track your progress.

A diary can help to re-motivate you as you look back through all the other fitness improvements you have made.

When losing weight you may find that over the first six weeks of training you lose 10kg/22lb but then you don't lose any in the seventh week, which can lessen your motivation. However, it's not just the weight loss that matters; for example, if you have been walking in an effort to accelerate your weight loss, and could only walk for 1.6km/1 mile in your first week, but can now manage 4.8km/3 miles, this progress will motivate you to keep going.

If you are training for a marathon, keep a diary of all your training, including details such as whether your training is road or off-road running, the time of day, your nutrition and hours of sleep. This way, if you do suffer from any problems, such as an overuse injury, a coach or physician will be able to use your diary to see when the problems may have started and may be able to determine what caused them. Noting what you eat will help you determine which foods work best for your performance and recovery.

Above: By taking your measurements, you can work out that you have lost fat and are more toned than before.

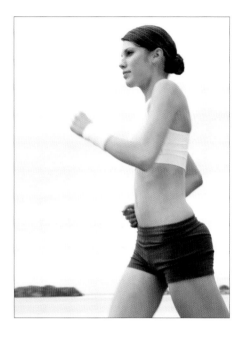

Above: If you step up your walking, note the details in your diary, to allow you to assess your progress better.

How to keep your training diary

You should record details of your training, the goals you want to achieve and an assessment of your training to date. Include test results, nutrition information and body measurements.

Daily records Record the following information in your diary every day:

• The physical training you intend to do against the actual physical training that took place, marked out of ten.

• Hours of sleep the previous night.

• Resting heart rate, taken first thing in the morning.

• Any injury or signs of fatigue.

• All food and fluid intake, including what time you ate or drank.

Also note what you did on rest days, as your activity on these days will have a significant effect on your performance. For example, if you stayed up late on a rest day, or drank alcohol on two rest days before a big competition, your performance will suffer and when you check the diary you will know why.

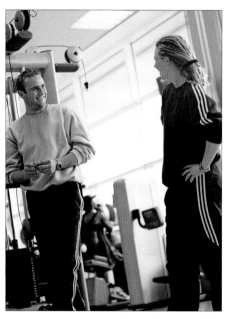

Above: Your training needs to work the way you want it to. You can discuss your progress with an instructor at the gym.

Big goals and small goals At the front of your diary list the goals you want to achieve, and when you want to achieve them by. For example, if you weigh 70kg/154lb on 1 January and you want to lose 10.8kg/24lb over six months, or 1.8kg/4lb per month, mark your desired weight – your small goal – on the appropriate page for each month; so on the page for 1 February, you would note that you want to weigh 68kg/150lb, and on the page for 1 March, you would note that you want to weigh 66kg/146lb, and so on.

Weekly assessment At the end of each week assess how your training has gone. Note the average score you have given to your training and how you felt each day. Look back over your nutrition for the week and mark down any changes you want to make. Assess your fluid intake for the week and check that you are drinking enough. Add up the total number of hours you have been

Below left: Note any injury; what you were doing and for how long. It may help you alter your training plan.

Below middle: An accurately filled-in training diary can prove to be an invaluable asset at a later date.

Below right: Keep a record of the hours that you sleep to get an insight into your sleeping patterns.

training and compare it with the week before. Make a note of measurements such as body fat, weight and Body Mass Index (BMI).

Weekly review If the overview of your week is not positive, consider where you may have gone wrong and note the changes that you intend to make in order to get more from your training. These changes might involve a different combination of exercises, taking more

Above: Even if your goal seems daunting at times, try to meet the challenge and stay on track.

rest days or working harder to achieve intensity levels in certain sessions. Look back at the goals you have set yourself, written at the front of the diary, and make changes to the small goals – adding new ones and ticking off the ones that you have achieved.

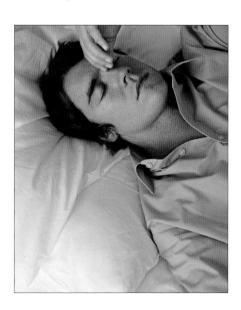

Body Measurements

There are many different ways of measuring your body on a regular basis and assessing your progress. As you see your body shape gradually but definitely changing, it will help to give you the motivation you need to keep training.

The weighing scales are one of the oldest but most effective ways of recording your weight. Always use the same scales to weigh yourself at the same time of the day, on the same day of the week. Place the scales in the same place on a hard floor each time to get a true measure. If your goal is to lose weight, only weigh yourself once a week to give yourself a chance to see the weight decrease. Weighing yourself first thing in the morning will reduce the chance of the measure being affected by what you have eaten, as you probably won't have eaten anything for at least 8 hours. However, dehydration after a heavy night of drinking alcohol can make you seem lighter on the scales, so don't be fooled by this.

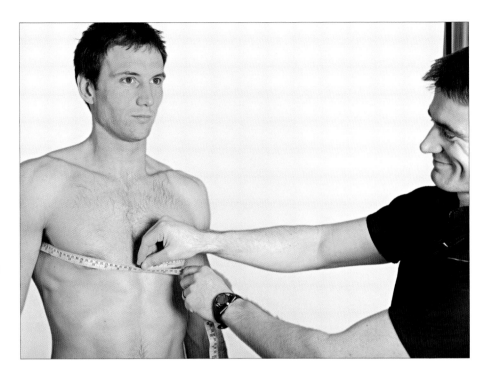

Measuring tape
A measuring tape is another useful way of monitoring your progress. Take measurements once a week at the same time as weighing yourself. Measure several different areas of the body each week. Breathe normally and don't suck your belly in when you measure.

Below: Scales don't always tell the whole story. You may have changed shape, but muscle is heavier than fat.

Above: Using a tape measure is an accurate indicator that your fitness regime is working well.

If the scales don't show a change in weight, the measuring tape might be your saviour. If your measurements are reducing, you know you are going in the right direction, even if you haven't lost weight. This change in shape and weight may be a result of more training, as muscle weighs more than fat – in fact, the same volume of muscle weighs nearly twice as much as the same volume of fat.

Use your body measurements to create your long- and short-term goals, but remember to be realistic. If you are trying to lose weight and your waist measures 102cm/40in, set a goal to lose 1cm/½in every two weeks until you reach your end goal of a 81cm/32in waist. If you are trying to gain muscle and change body shape, and your chest is 97cm/38in, set targets of a 2.5cm/1in increase in size until you reach your goal.

How to measure yourself

Chest: measure around the body, in line with the nipples.

Waist: measure around the body, in line with the belly button.

Hips: measure around the widest part of the hips.

Thighs: measure around the leg 15cm/6in up from the top of the knee.

Calves: measure around the mid-point of the lower leg.

Biceps: measure around the mid-point of the upper arm (decide whether you want to do this with the muscle tensed or with a straight arm, and use the same method of measurement each time so that you will be able to record any differences accurately).

Shoulders: measure from the middle of the side of one shoulder across the back to the middle of the side of the other shoulder.

Neck: measure around the mid-point of the neck.

Photographs and mirrors

One of the best ways to measure your progress is to look in the mirror and assess what you see. Obviously, you will not be able to remember what you see from one week to the next, so take photographs to compare the difference. This is especially important if you are trying to lose weight, change body shape or put on muscle mass. You can also use the mirror to assess your muscle definition if you are trying to put on muscle and look leaner. If you use a tape measure to measure your biceps, and the measurements don't change from week six to eight but the mirror and photographs show a distinct change in appearance, you will be instantly motivated to continue training. If you have been working on your running technique for your next 10km/6.2-mile race or marathon, run in front of the mirror or use photographs or a camcorder to see the difference in your technique.

Using a mirror for most weight-training exercises, especially with free weights, is essential. You need constantly to check whether you are using the right technique. Many people use weights that are too heavy for them and so fail to work the correct muscles, because the

Below: By regularly examining your body in a mirror, you will notice any areas that look different.

Above: If you have photographs taken at intervals, you will easily be able to see any bodily changes.

weight forces them to use other parts of their body instead of isolating the muscles they really want to work.

Clothes that fit

How your clothes fit is one of the best measures of your progress. The scales and the tape measure may at times suggest that your body has not changed at all, but if you go down a dress, trouser or shirt size, you will be inspired to continue training – it clearly is working. Clothes can tell you more than any measuring tape; for example, it is hard to use a measuring tape to measure the size of the buttocks but if your trousers feel looser, then obviously you have become thinner – in that area

Above: How your clothes fit is a good indicator of losing body fat. After weight loss, they feel much looser.

at least. Buy clothes that you want to fit into in the future, and use this as a small goal on the path to achieving your goal.

Above: If you are prepared to put in the required effort, you will achieve the results you want.

Measuring Body Fat

If you are trying to gain weight in the form of muscle, and you are eating more and taking supplements, measuring body fat regularly will help you to see whether you are gaining muscle or fat, and keep you on track to reach your goals.

As already stated at the beginning of this book, fad diets simply don't work. Many of them, in fact, can result in a higher percentage of body fat because a diet that leads to fast results often causes you to lose just as much muscle as fat. This reduction in muscle means that your metabolism will be lower, and as a result you will put on more fat, especially after the diet has come to an end – which, invariably, it will.

If your weight on the scales is the same as before you started the diet, but your body fat has dropped from 15 to 10 per cent, you will know that you have gained a considerable amount of muscle.

Below: Don't be discouraged if you are not losing weight quickly; slow and steady ensures it stays off.

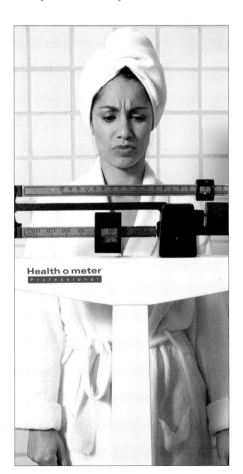

Body fat table			

Once you have calculated your body fat, compare your percentage with the figures on this table. You should try to stay within these boundaries – having some fat is essential for regulating the body's temperature and protecting vital organs.

Age	up to 30 years old	30–50 years old	50+ years old
Female	14–21 per cent	15–21 per cent	16–25 per cent
Male	9–15 per cent	11–17 per cent	12–19 per cent

How to measure body fat

There are several different ways to measure body fat. The most accurate is hydrostatic weighing, which works by submerging the subject in a tank and measuring the water that is displaced. It is one of the most reliable tests, as factors such as how much fluid has been drunk in the last hour will not affect the results. However, you are unlikely to have a suitable tank at home and you won't find one at many sports clubs either. Instead, you are more likely to encounter body-fat scales and callipers.

A set of body-fat measuring scales will give you a rough estimate of your body fat. A low level electrical current is passed through the body and the impedance (opposition to the flow of current) is measured. The result is used with your weight and other factors to give you a body fat percentage. However, your body's impedance level can be affected by the amount of water in your body, any recent exercise and your skin temperature. If you are going to use body-fat scales to measure body fat don't eat or drink for at least 3 hours before measuring and avoid exercise for 12 hours before measuring.

Using body-fat callipers is more accurate if the same person does the measuring each time; the same amount of skin is pinched; the same side of the body is measured (usually the right-hand side); and the same equation is used to calculate body fat. If you repeat the same test in a month's time, and your fat percentage has gone down, you know your training plan is working. There are a few rules you should stick to:

- The same person should measure you every time.
- Measure at the same time of day.

Below: This woman is having her fat measured in a hydrostatic weighing pool, which is a very accurate method.

Body fat by sport
Average body-fat percentage for athletes.

Sport	male	female
Baseball	12–15	12–18
Basketball	6–12	20–27
Football	9–19	15–30
Cross-country running	5–12	12–18
Tennis	12–16	16–24
Triathlon	5–12	10–15

- Avoid drinking and eating for at least 3 hours before measurement.
- Avoid exercise for at least 12 hours before measuring.
- Hold the skin fold between the thumb and the index finger.
- Apply the callipers at a depth equal to the thickness of the fold.
- Repeat the measurement three times and take an average, so that you get an accurate reading.
- Add the readings for the different areas of the body together and use the equations that follow.

Instead of converting your skin-fold measurements into an actual body-fat reading, you could just add up your skin-fold measurements and use this to determine whether you are losing or gaining fat. If you want to focus on one area, such as losing weight from your stomach, then simply take one skin-fold measure from your abdomen using the following method. With a thumb and finger, pick up a skin fold with two thicknesses of skin and subcutaneous fat. Grip the skin with the callipers 1cm/½in from the fingers, at a depth the same thickness as the skin fold.

Measurements
Remember that muscle weighs more than fat so if the reading on the scales doesn't change don't feel defeatist. To check if you are losing fat, take body measurements using a tape measure, measure your skin folds with callipers and use your mirror to see the changes. Use your scales only twice a week unless you are an athlete in training.

How to calculate body-fat percentage
Specially calibrated callipers that grip the skin and fat are used for the measurement; three readings are taken at each site and an average is used for the calculation of body fat.

Triceps: *the back of the arm located halfway between the shoulder and the elbow. Measure vertically.*

Sub scapular: *situated just below the shoulder blade. Measure at a 45-degree angle.*

Supraspinale: *on the side of the abdomen just below the line of the belly button. Measure horizontally.*

Abdominal area: *this is just beside the belly button. Measure the fat vertically.*

Thigh: *at the midpoint of the front of the thigh. Measure vertically.*

Calf: *taken at the back of the largest part of the calf. Measure vertically.*

Calculate your body-fat percentage using an equation such as this:
Equation for males: percentage body fat = (0.1051 x sum of triceps, sub scapular, supraspinale, abdominal, thigh and calf) + 2.585
Equation for females: percentage body fat = (0.1545 x sum of triceps, sub scapular, supraspinale, abdominal, thigh and calf) + 3.580
Yuhasz, M.S., *Physical Fitness Manual*, University of Western Ontario, 1974

Body Mass Index and Health Measurements

While the Body Mass Index is generally a useful way to assess whether your body mass is obese, overweight, normal or underweight, it is not always a straightforward measure, depending on who you are. It pays, therefore, to understand it in some detail.

Body Mass Index (BMI) is a measure of a person's weight scaled according to their height (see box 'Measuring your BMI'). This parameter is a useful tool for monitoring your progress in health and fitness. However, it is not accurate in all cases. For example, power athletes may have the same BMI score as an overweight person, even though they are carrying no fat. The reason for this is that the BMI does not account for the amount of lean muscle the athlete is carrying. Likewise, many endurance athletes have a BMI score indicating that they are underweight, even though they are actually a healthy weight. In older people, BMI

Measuring your BMI
Use the following methods to find your BMI:

Metric
BMI = body mass in kilograms/divided by height x height in meters

Example:
A 1.78m tall person, weighing 79.83kg would have a BMI of 25:
79.83kg/(1.78 x 1.78)
= 79.83/3.16
= 25

Imperial
BMI = body mass in pounds/divided by height x height in inches multiplied by 703

Example:
A 5ft 10in (70in) tall person, weighing 176lb would have a BMI of 25:
176lb/(70 x 70) x 703
= 176/4,900 x 703
= 25

Above: Muscular people may have a higher BMI. This does not, however, mean that they are unhealthy.

Right: Long-distance runners who are lightweight will generally have a low BMI.

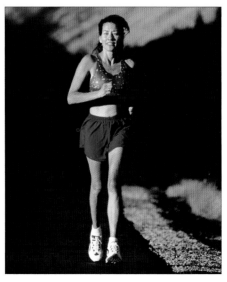

readings may be of little use, as they will not take into account loss of muscle mass. Neither can the BMI be an accurate measure for children or breastfeeding mothers. However, those exceptions aside, the BMI provides a good basic guideline to follow for the general population.

How to measure your waist-to-hip ratio

Take your waist measurement by measuring round your body at the midpoint between the bottom of your waist and hips. Measure your hips by measuring around your body where your buttocks stick out the most. Divide your waist measurement by your hip measurement. For example, a 81cm/32in waist and 102cm/40in hip would be calculated as a waist-to-hip ratio of 0.8. This ratio is reasonable for a man but is the upper limit for a woman.

Above: To measure your waist, hold the tape measure between the lower part of the waist and the hips.

Above: The hips are measured by holding the tape measure at the widest place.

Blood pressure

If your blood pressure is higher than 140/100, you should consult a doctor before you start any exercise routine. It is easy to measure blood pressure yourself with a blood pressure monitor that you can buy from larger pharmacies. It is best to take the test before you have done any exercise that day, as that may affect the result. However, if you have already exercised, then make sure that you rest for at least 30 minutes before you take a reading.

Cholesterol

Your doctor can check your cholesterol level by a simple blood test. The result is reported in millimoles per litre (mmol/l) or milligrams per decilitre (mg/dl). A cholesterol level of 5 mmol/l/200mg/dl or less is desirable, 5 to 6 is borderline, and above 6 puts you at a high risk of a heart attack. In the UK, 75 per cent of adults aged over 40 have a level higher than 5, and 54 per cent of heart attacks are linked with levels of over 5.

Waist-to-hip ratio

Other body measurements are also useful for monitoring health. Simply measuring your waist and hips, then calculating your waist-to-hip ratio, can be just as effective as the BMI measurement for highlighting health risk factors, especially for heart disease

Below: There is no need to visit the doctor to take your blood pressure; you can easily measure it yourself.

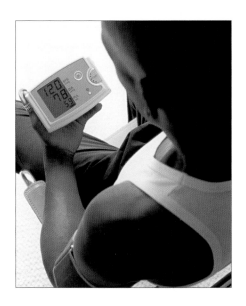

and type II diabetes, as it has been proven that people who carry excess fat around their middle are more at risk of these illnesses.

The risk of health problems has been found to increase if a man has a waist measurement of over 102cm/40in, or a woman has a waist measurement of more than 89cm/35in. A waist-to-hip ratio of more than 1 for men and 0.8 for women is highly detrimental to your health. At this point, the risk of heart disease, hypertension and type II diabetes is dramatically increased.

Above: The amount you can firmly pinch indicates extra weight and also the state of your wellbeing.

BMI and health risks

Studies show that the BMI score is linked to health risk factors. Compare your score with those on the chart below. If your health risk is high or very high, you should consult a doctor and start taking exercise and eating sensibly immediately.

BMI score	Classification	Health risk
Less than 18.5	underweight	moderate
18.5–24.9	normal	very low
25–29.9	overweight	low
30–34.9	obese class 1	moderate
35–39.9	obese class 2	high
Above 40	extreme obesity	very high

Cardiovascular Fitness Tests

It is essential when following a training programme that you test your cardiovascular fitness, and there are a number of ways you can do this. It is equally important that the test you choose is appropriate to the sport you will be doing.

Tests vary depending on the sport and the first step when testing your cardiovascular fitness is selecting the right test for you and your sport. If you are a sprinter, you need to set yourself tests on the track covering the distances, or similar distances, that you will be running in competition. Testing yourself over 5km/3 miles will be of little use to you.

If you are a cyclist, test your fitness with a 8km/5-mile or 16km/10-mile time trial over a familiar route – one that you can use in the future for comparison.

For invasion sports such as basketball or netball, test yourself by running different lengths of the court and timing

Measuring up

When testing your fitness, use a treadmill or run on an athletics track so that you can easily measure your distance.

The VO2 max table fitness assessment

Female

Age	Very poor	Poor	Fair	Good	Excellent	Superior
13–19	<25	25–30.9	31–34.9	35–38.9	39–41.9	>41.9
20–29	<23.6	23.6–28.9	29–32.9	33–36.9	37–41	>41
30–39	<22.8	22.8–26.9	27–31.4	31.5–35.6	35.7–40	>40
40–49	<21	21–24.4	24.5–28.9	29–32.8	32.9–36.9	>36.9
50–59	<20.2	20.2–22.7	22.8–26.9	27–31.4	31.5–35.7	>35.7
60+	<17.5	17.7–20.1	20.2–24.4	24.5–30.2	30.3–31.4	>31.4

Male

Age	Very poor	Poor	Fair	Good	Excellent	Superior
13–19	<35–36	36–38	38.4–45.1	45.2–50.9	51.0–55.9	>55.9
20–29	<33.0	33.0–36.4	36.5–42.4	42.5–46.4	46.5–52.4	>52.4
30–39	<31.5	31.5–35.4	35.5–40.9	41.0–44.0	45.0–49.4	>49.4
40–49	<30.2	30.2–33.5	33.6–38.9	39.0–43.7	43.8–48.0	>48.0
50–59	<26.1	26.1–30.9	31.0–35.7	35.8–40.9	41.0–45.3	>45.3
60+	<20.5	20.5–26.0	26.1–32.2	32.3–36.4	36.5–44.2	>44.2

Cooper, K.H., *The Physical Fitness Specialist Certification Manual*, The Cooper Institute for Aerobics Research, Dallas, Texas, 1968

Below: Sprinting demands a fast delivery of oxygen to your muscles. This is known as 'aerobic exercise'.

Below: If you enter a triathlon, you need to ensure that you do regular cardiovascular training.

Below: Games require a fast, efficient cardiovascular system to enable rapid recovery between points.

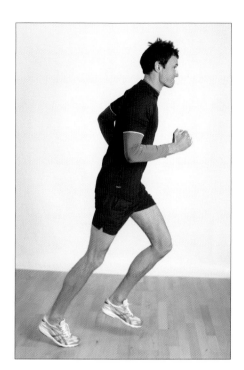

Above: If you have a high level of fitness attempt the Cooper 12-minute run test, in which you run or walk for 12 minutes.

yourself. Try starting at the back of the court and running to the halfway mark and back five times, and then running to the far end of the court and back five times and getting an overall time.

For rowing, set a distance such as 2,000m/2,187yd and time yourself. Then test yourself again in the future to check for fitness improvements.

There are three useful measurements that test either aerobic fitness or the cardiovascular system: the VO2 max, the Cooper 12-minute run and the Harvard step test.

VO2 max The VO2 max test measures the maximum volume of oxygen (O_2) that an athlete can use during intense exercise. The test is suitable for elite athletes who are able to push

Repeatable test

Only use a fitness test that will be easy for you to repeat. You should note your fitness test results in your training diary and repeat the tests every four to six weeks to monitor your improvement and help determine if your training is working for you. If you are training correctly you will see a change.

themselves hard without risk of injury or other health problems. It is also one of the best measures of cardiovascular fitness because it shows you how efficient your body is at utilizing oxygen and represents your maximum aerobic capacity. It is expressed as ml/kg/min (millilitres of oxygen per kilogram of body weight per minute).

The most accurate way to test VO2 max is to exercise to failure (when you reach the point that you simply cannot push your body any further) and use laboratory techniques to work out the exact amount of oxygen you are able to utilize by measuring the air that you exhale. However, there is a simple test you can do to predict your VO2 max without using specialist equipment, and which does not involve exercising to complete failure:

The Cooper 12-minute run Like the VO2 max, this test is also suitable for elite athletes used to pushing themselves hard. It measures the body's ability to use oxygen while running. Run or walk as far as possible in 12 minutes, then measure the distance in metres/yards to predict your VO2 max. Use the following formula to calculate your estimated VO2 max in ml/kg/min (milligrams of oxygen/ kilogram body weight/minute):

Miles: VO2 max=35.97 x miles - 11.29
Kilometers: VO2 max=22.4 x km - 11.3

An endurance athlete, such as a marathon runner would generally have a high VO2 of around 70ml/kg/min, an average level would be 35 and a poor level is 25 or below.

The Harvard step test Anyone who wants to get fit can use the Harvard step test, which monitors the cardiovascular system. This is a basic test that involves stepping up on to a 40–50cm/16–20in high gym bench once every 2 seconds for 5 minutes and recording your heart rate. Note your heart rate 1 minute after finishing the test (HR1), again after 2 minutes (HR2) and, finally, again after 3 minutes (HR3). Use the following calculation to assess the state of your fitness:

The Harvard step test results

>90	excellent
80–89	good
65–79	above average
55–64	below average
<55	poor

McArdle, W.D. et al, *Physiology: Energy, Nutrition and Human Performance,* 1991.

Fitness level = 30,000/2 x (HR1 + HR2 + HR3). For example, 30,000/2 x (120 + 100 + 80) = 50.

A high level of 80 or 90 is good, indicating a healthy cardiovascular system, while 50 or below is poor. Before you attempt any form of cardiovascular test for the first time, you should consult your doctor. Always have somebody with you during the test.

Below: The Harvard step test is a way of noting your heart rate to assess your state of fitness.

Equipment for Cardiovascular Training

Before you use cardiovascular equipment, in the gym or at home, you need to take into account a number of important factors. These include, location, space, value, safety, hygiene, familiarity with the controls and, most of all, using machinery that 'fits' you.

Whether you decide to train at home or in a public gym, the location and its surroundings are very important. The place you choose for your training must be somewhere that you really want to go. It must be somewhere to look forward to, especially if you are going to train after a long day's work. If you are going to join a public gym, there are a number of factors to consider.

Gym conditions

Always check the level of instruction on offer at the gym. Find out whether the instructors are qualified, and to what level. Find out how much help is on offer. If you have not used a gym before, you will need all the help you can get to set up machinery and feel safe with what you are doing. There also needs to

Below: Understanding the equipment will make your workout more enjoyable and useful.

be plenty of natural light or, failing that, good-quality artificial lighting and ventilation to keep you supplied with plentiful fresh air. Air-conditioning will help to cool you down, but it may lead to greater dehydration, especially during cardiovascular exercise, so take care to carry a drinks bottle with you at all times.

Spend some time at the gym before you join and study closely what it is like at different times of the day. It may be very quiet on your first visit at 10 a.m., but it may be packed with people waiting to use the machines at 6 p.m. – the very time you are most likely to want to train, if you have a regular job. Make sure, too, that the machines are kept in good order and are hygienic.

The machines that you will be using for cardiovascular training include treadmills, exercise bikes, cross-trainers, rowing machines, steppers, trampolines and vibration plates.

Measuring up and splashing out

You may not feel like using the gym close to you; a gym environment is not ideal for everyone, in which case, you should consider training at home, but check carefully the amount of space you have, and the access, before ordering any unnecessary gym equipment. For cross-trainers and treadmills, you will need considerable ceiling height. Buying cardiovascular equipment can be very expensive. It doesn't have be the most state-of-the-art to be useful to you but, generally, the more costly it is, the more functional and robust it will be. If you want to work out using smooth machinery with lots of built-in cardiovascular programmes, then spend more money. Many manufacturers describe

their cardiovascular equipment as being for 'domestic use' or 'commercial use'. The commercial use equipment will be more expensive, but it will last longer because it is designed for continual heavy use in a public gym.

Below: The heart-rate monitor is worn around the chest, over the heart. A reading can be seen on the wrist device.

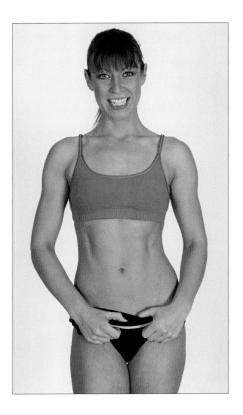

Above: It is essential to wear a supportive sports bra when doing vigorous training.

Above: Always check your equipment for safety. For hygiene, wear only your own boxing gloves.

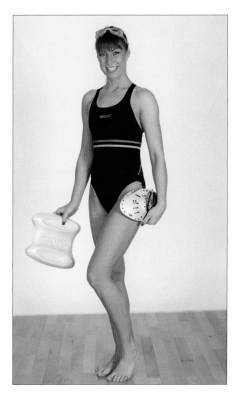

Above: Swimming aids such as floats and pull buoys will help to improve your technique.

From treadmills to rowing machines, the choice of cardiovascular equipment is endless. If you can afford it and have the space, have at least two pieces of cardiovascular equipment so that you can vary your exercise routine. There should be a number of programmes to stop you getting bored. Also, keep in mind that treadmills have different maximum speeds and levels of incline. Rowers use different pulley mechanisms, while cross-trainers vary in size and motion. Some stationary bikes are more adjustable than others. Try out the equipment before you buy and make sure the machine is right for you.

Heart-rate monitor
Constantly use a heart-rate monitor to analyse your training efforts. Most good heart-rate monitors allow you to set zones for your desired level of intensity. You can buy more expensive versions that allow you to download the data to your PC and copy the workout data into a diary, if you wish. However, being able to view your heart rate easily during your training session is the most important factor. Make sure that your

---

Divert and motivate
Distractions when you are doing cardiovascular exercise are good. Use an MP3 player or watch television to turn your routine into a pleasant experience and make the time go faster. Knowing that you can watch a favourite TV programme may motivate you to get to the gym.

---

heart-rate monitor is coded so that it only picks up a signal from you and not your training partner's signal.

Clothing
For running, rowing or other similar cardiovascular exercise, wear loose-fitting, lightweight, breathable clothing. Always wear good footwear with plenty of support and cushioning. Females should wear good-quality supportive tops to prevent them feeling uncomfortable or self-conscious in front of others.

For boxing, it is essential to always have the correct protective pads and gloves. For hygiene reasons, always try to use your own gloves in a public gym. If you do have to use other

---

people's gloves, remember to wash your hands thoroughly afterward. Remove all your jewellery and watches to prevent injuries.

For swimming, wear a well-fitted swimming costume that is supportive but will allow you to move with maximum efficiency through the water. Use pull buoys and floats to help you improve your swimming technique. Choose goggles that attach firmly to your face with suction before you've even put the strap around your head. This is the sign of a good fit; wearing loose goggles when swimming are next to useless; they will allow water to get into your eyes, and will only interfere with the smooth timing, enjoyment and effectiveness of your session.

Suitable equipment
If you are training outdoors, always take a pack with the necessary clothing, including waterproof outerwear, and sun cream, when appropriate. Also, remember to take with you a water bottle, other drinks and snacks.

CARDIOVASCULAR TRAINING

Any form of exercise that raises your heartbeat is cardiovascular, whether it is walking to the shops or swimming a long distance. What matters is finding the exercise that suits you best and slowly building up your level of intensity in order to achieve your goals. At the outset, you do not need to suffer to feel the benefits. However, to challenge your body, make it fun and get the best results, include variety in your training, and keep a record of your exercise to monitor your progress and stay motivated.

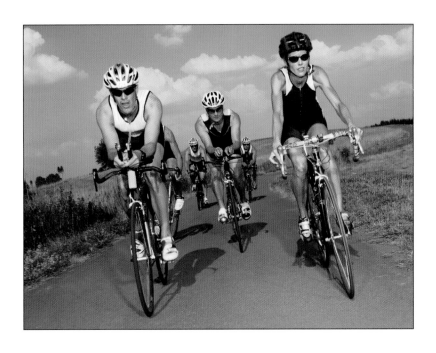

Above: Training in groups can make fitness fun.
Left: Running can be enjoyable, as well as helping you to achieve fitness.

The Benefits of Cardiovascular Exercise

Whether you are planning to run a marathon, take part in a triathlon or simply improve your general health and fitness to deal better with everyday demands, cardiovascular training has the added advantage of promoting your wellbeing.

Cardiovascular exercise has a beneficial effect on the body. It will promote weight loss and enable your heart and lungs to work more efficiently and become stronger. It will help to increase bone density, reduce stress and decrease the risk of heart disease and some cancers, particularly colon, prostrate and breast cancer. Regular cardiovascular exercise relieves depression, increases your level of confidence, improves your sleep patterns and gives you more energy to combat challenges at home and at work. It can help to lower cholesterol, triglyceride (fat in the bloodstream and fat tissue) and blood pressure levels. Glucose tolerance (how your body breaks down blood sugar) and insulin sensitivity (how well the insulin in the body controls blood sugar levels) will also improve. For athletic performance, the more cardiovascular exercise you do, the faster your heart rate will recover, and metabolize glucose to give your muscles the energy they need.

Below: The cardiovascular system consists of the heart and a closed system of arteries, veins and capillaries. Because the heart and lungs are made from muscular tissue, they need to be trained, just like other muscles.

Lung   Heart   Lung

Appropriate exercises
Different exercises will benefit different people, depending on their fitness level and injuries. For example, a big muscular person will benefit more from rowing, in which there is no impact and they can use a large amount of muscle mass. Running, however, involves constant impact and is more likely to cause injury. It relies on the legs to carry the weight and doesn't use the upper-body muscles.

Losing weight
• To achieve weight loss and maintain your new lower weight, you must combine cardiovascular training with resistance training, because resistance training will increase your muscle metabolism and help you to burn more calories.
• To lose weight, do exercises that use greater muscle mass. The rowing machine and the cross-trainer work both your upper and lower body and will burn more calories compared to other cardiovascular exercises.

Above: Boxing provides a complete workout for your cardiovascular and endurance systems.

Enjoy yourself Choose a cardiovascular activity that you enjoy, so that you'll want to do more of it. If you dread going to the gym, try training with a partner, perhaps competing side by side on a bike or doing some boxercise. Use music to distract yourself from the exercise, especially if you are exercising at low intensity to burn fat. To motivate yourself before a training session, think about how great you will feel after you have completed a good cardiovascular session – energized, fresh and stress free.
Challenge yourself If you run for 5km/ 3 miles on the treadmill every other day, your body will soon get used to this exercise, and the lack of challenge will result in fewer calories being burnt and only a small improvement to your fitness level. Rather than doing the same exercise at the same level of intensity, combine different exercises and levels of intensity all the time to give your body new

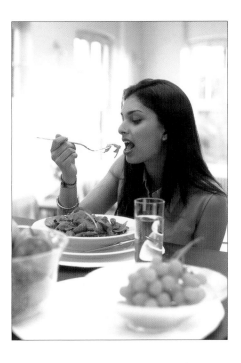

Above: Eat a healthy, nutritious diet to prepare for and recover from cardiovascular workouts.

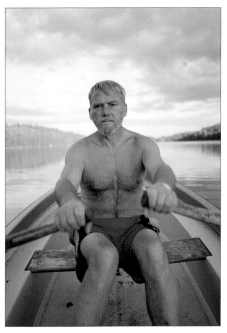

Above: Rowing trains your cardiovascular system without the impact of running.

Above: Make running a more challenging experience by trying out different surfaces and terrains.

challenges. For example, run for about 3 minutes at a steady pace, then accelerate and hold a fast pace for the fourth minute, before returning to a steady pace. When out walking, adjust

Below: Weights alone will not benefit your cardiovascular system – you need a mixture of different types of exercise.

your training route to include more hills to challenge your body and increase your heart rate, thereby making you work harder to achieve fitness.

When to train

Everybody has a preferred time of day to train. If you train first thing in the morning before eating, you will burn

straight into your fat stores as your glycogen stores (stored glucose, mainly in the muscles and liver), which you usually use in the first 20 minutes of exercise, will have depleted overnight. If you follow resistance training with cardiovascular training, you will also burn straight into fat stores. This may seem like a more efficient way of burning fat but be careful – you may start to feel dizzy and you may even pass out if your glycogen levels are low. Training will increase your energy level, so you may want to train during your lunch break so that you have greater energy for the afternoon's work.

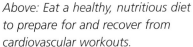

Training tips
• To start burning fat, your exercise regime should last for at least 20 minutes.
• To feel the maximum benefits of cardiovascular exercise, you should train at least three times a week at between 60 and 90 per cent of your maximum heart rate.
• Elite athletes need to train at between 75 and 95 per cent of their maximum heart rate if they want to make significant fitness improvements.

Cardiovascular Energy Expenditure

When estimating the number of calories you will burn in an exercise session, you need to take into account duration, speed and intensity of exercise, along with your body type and the muscle requirement of each exercise.

The longer you exercise, the more calories you will burn. If you are unfit, you should exercise at a lower intensity so that you can exercise for longer before fatigue sets in. For example, if you are trying to run for the first time, begin by alternating 1 minute of jogging with 3 minutes of walking, then repeating for as long as possible. If you attempt to jog continuously, the chances are that you will last less

Below: Boxing is extremely demanding, and around just 3 minutes of hard boxing can seem a very long time.

than 10 minutes. By alternating walking and jogging, you may be able to last for up to 1 hour.

Speed of exercise

The faster the exercise, the more calories you burn. Going faster will force your body to work harder, and muscle cells to contract faster. You have to burn more calories to maintain a fast work rate.

Intensity level

The greater the intensity of the exercise, the higher the number of calories you will burn. Intense exercise will not only

Above: If you constantly paddle out, catch a wave and surf in again, you will burn more calories.

burn calories during exercise, it will also make you burn more calories after the exercise has stopped. Interval training and sprinting will have this afterburn effect because your muscles need energy to recover, which in turn burns more calories.

Body type

Mesomorphs are naturally leaner and possess more metabolically active muscle cells. This means that they will have a higher metabolic rate, even at rest, and will, therefore, burn a greater number of calories, further helping them to stay lean.

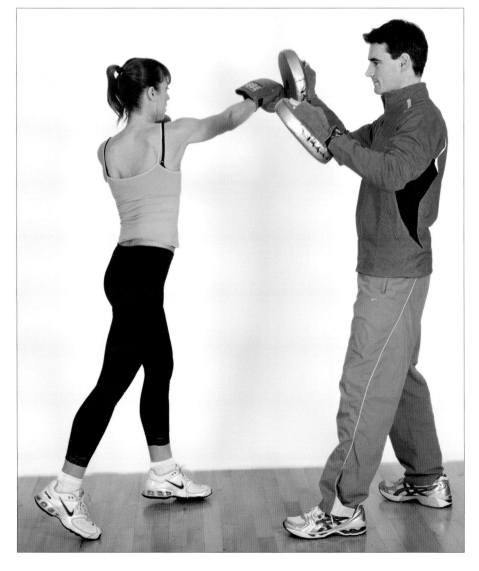

Appropriate nutrition

If you are quite lean already, make sure that your food intake is sufficient to keep up with your exercise demands. If it is not, you may be forced to break down muscle to provide energy. In the long term, this means less muscle mass and, therefore, a reduced potential for burning calories.

Above: Cycling at speed uses up a lot of calories and they continue to burn even after the exercise has stopped.

The heavier a person is, the more calories he or she is likely to burn during exercise because they have got more weight to move around. For example, the energy required for a runner who weighs 63kg/140lb is far less than the energy needed for a runner who weighs 90kg/200lb, or almost twice as much. The lighter runner burns off fewer calories.

Below: For someone of average weight, baseball burns up around 350 calories in 1 hour.

Muscle use

There is a simple equation to keep in mind when it comes to exercise and calorie burn. Exercises that involve using greater amounts of muscle will burn more calories. For example, a training session on the rowing machine will burn more calories than a similar session on a static bike because rowing uses both your upper and lower body. However, cycling, when riding at speed, may burn up a lot of calories, even though it uses only your leg muscles. Competitive sports require high-speed running or sprinting and can burn off hundreds of calories in an hour.

Calorie burn by exercise

The following list shows an estimate of how many calories you can expect to burn in 1 hour of constant exercise, depending on your body weight, and the speed you are going at, for a variety of popular sports and activities.

Exercise	59kg/130lb	70kg/155lb	86kg/190lb
Aerobics, general	354	422	518
Aerobics, high impact	413	493	604
American football	593	783	866
Baseball	295	352	431
Basketball	472	563	690
Cycling <16kph/10mph	236	281	345
Cycling >32kph/20mph	944	1,126	1380
Cycling, mountain bike	502	598	733
Boxercise	531	633	776
Rowing, racing	708	844	1035
Rowing, leisure	177	211	259
Dancing, fast	325	387	474
Dancing, slow	177	211	259
Football	531	633	776
Golf	236	281	345
Handball	472	563	690
Hockey	472	563	690
Horse riding	236	281	345
Ice hockey	340	485	592
Rugby	590	704	863
Running 16kph/10mph	944	1,126	1,380
Running 13kph/8mph	796	950	1,165
Running 10kph/6mph	590	704	863
Ice-skating	413	493	604
Skateboarding	340	495	604
Skiing, cross-country	826	985	1,208
Skiing, downhill	354	422	518
Skiing, water	354	422	518
Squash	708	844	1,035
Surfing	177	211	259
Swimming, fast	590	704	863
Swimming, leisure	354	422	518
Tennis, singles	472	563	690
Tennis, doubles	354	422	518
Volleyball	472	563	690
Walking 6kph/4mph	236	281	345
Walking 5kph/3mph	207	246	302
Walking 3kph/2mph	148	176	216
Weightlifting	354	422	518

Heart Rate

The heart circulates oxygenated blood from your lungs to the working muscles. Using a heart-rate monitor will help to monitor the stresses you are putting on your heart and will reduce the risk of injury and overtraining.

Your heart rate is measured in beats per minute (bpm). You can measure your heart rate by using the pulse on your wrist or neck and counting the number of pulses in 6 seconds and then multiplying it by ten. However, the best way to monitor your heart rate is to use a heart-rate monitor. It's easy to use: simply place the strap around your torso just underneath the top of your chest or

HRZ

To train safely and effectively, you need to establish your correct heart rate zone (HRZ) for the various training levels. To do this, you first need to calculate your heart resting rate (HRR), using this formula:

HRR = maximum heart rate (MHR) − resting heart rate (RHR)

Calculating HRR

220bpm (MHR) − 60bpm (RHR) = 160bpm (HRR)

Your HRZ can be set using percentages of your HRR, using this formula:

HRZ = (HRR x percentage level of intensity) + RHR

Use the formula to work out your heart rate zone (HRZ) for all your training levels of intensity. Most heart-rate monitors will have a facility to set training zones. The watch will flash or make a noise if you go above or below the appropriate zone.

Calculating HRZ (Level 3 high intensity)

75–90 per cent (160 HRR x 75 per cent) + 60 RHR = 180bpm (bottom of L3) HRZ;

(160 HRR x 90 per cent) + 60 RHR = 204bpm HRZ (top of L3 HRZ).

bra line. The best time to measure resting heart rate (RHR) is first thing in the morning when you wake up – before the stresses of the day, eating and exercise can affect the reading. For an average reading, take your RHR every day for three days.

Heart rate can be used as a measure of how fit you are. The sooner your heart rate returns to its resting value after exercise – 55bpm for example – the fitter you are. It is worth monitoring your average heart rate (AHR) throughout similar exercise sessions to compare your fitness levels and keep you motivated. For example, if you regularly do a 4.8km/3-mile cycle ride in 15 minutes and your AHR reading is 155bpm, and you do the same bike ride a month later, in the same time, and your heart rate averages 145bpm, you know you are getting fitter.

Maximum heart rate

The maximum number of times your heart can contract in a minute is called the maximum heart rate (MHR). This is the best indicator to use to work out the intensity levels of your training. There are two methods to determine your MHR: the first involves increasing the intensity of exercises, step by step, over the space of 10–20 minutes until you reach total exhaustion. For example, ride the exercise bike at 16kph/10mph and increase the speed by 1.6kph/1mph every minute until you can't go any farther. You should not try this test unless you have a doctor with you, in case you have cardiac problems. The second method uses the following formula: MHR = 220 - your age.

Heart rate and health

You can use your heart rate to monitor your health and prevent yourself overtraining. If your RHR is five to ten beats higher than normal, this

Above: The strap of a heart-rate monitor, worn around the chest, sends information to the wrist monitor.

indicates that you may be coming down with an illness. You should, therefore, consider adjusting your training or taking a rest before you do any more damage. If your heart rate will not increase to the values you normally see when you are doing high-intensity

Below: The heart rate can easily be calculated by feeling for, and taking, your pulse.

Above: In the gym, many of the machines have heart-rate monitors built into the mechanism.

training, then you may be overtraining. Your body is telling you that it needs to rest – and you should listen to it.

Using your heart-rate monitor regularly in training sessions outdoors is a useful measure of how the weather conditions are affecting your performance. For example, if you are out on your normal cycle route and it is wet and windy, and you are cycling or running directly against the direction of the wind, you may find that you cover the ground slower. Your heart-rate monitor, however, tells you that you are working at the same intensity – if not higher – as you would if there were no wind. This shows that the wind is probably the limiting factor on your time. So, rather than overexerting yourself to beat your previous best time, and in the process increasing your risk of injury, use the heart-rate monitor to keep yourself in the correct zone. If you have not been exercising regularly or you are an athlete

returning from illness, consider using a heart-rate monitor to monitor your heart rate while exercising, that way you won't overdo your first few sessions on the way back to fitness. Avoid letting your heart rate go above 75 per cent of its maximum.

Above: Adverse weather conditions, such as rain or snow, can affect your heart rate.

Below: Cycling against a headwind slows you down and makes you work harder. This causes an increase in the heart rate.

Breathing Technique

There is an art to breathing correctly and getting the most out of each breath.
Good breathing technique will help lower blood pressure, purify the blood, increase
metabolism, improve digestion, promote rapid recovery after exercise and help you to relax.

Take a look at a gym full of people exercising and the chances are that you will notice most people resorting to shallow, fast breaths, because they are using only the top part of their chest to breathe. This type of breathing is inefficient and ineffective. Excessive panting is a waste of energy and does not deliver enough oxygen to your lungs. This rapid, shallow breathing may trigger what is known as a 'flight-or-flight' response: your heart rate increases as the heart pumps faster to use what little oxygen it has been given. This increases the stress on your body, which leads, in turn, to poor physical performance and increases the recovery time needed after your training session. Your brain is tricked into thinking you are exercising at high intensity when, in fact, if you were breathing correctly, you would be aware that it is not high intensity at all. Using only the top of the lungs with this type of short, shallow, chest breathing does not make use of the bottom half of your lungs, where

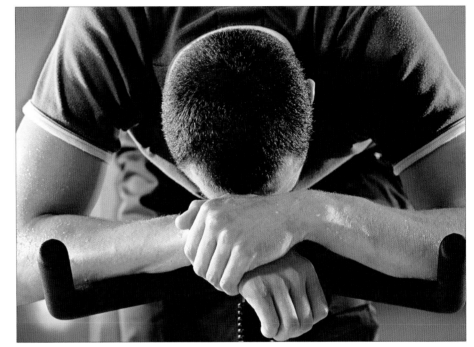

the most efficient exchange of oxygen takes place. It is important to exhale fully before you take in another breath or you simply won't have enough room for the new oxygen to come in.

Above: After strenuous exercise, you will feel less stressed and your recovery will be much quicker if you have been breathing correctly.

Shallow breathing

Diaphragm

Breathing exercises

During the week, try to regularly make time for some simple breathing exercises. Remember to keep your posture as upright as possible: relax your shoulders but keep your chest up and make sure your ears, shoulders and hips are all in line to maintain good posture.

If you add these two breathing exercises to your training plan twice a week, you will see the benefits within a few weeks.

Left: When breathing hard during exercise make sure you use the bottom half of the lungs to get maximum oxygen supply to your muscles. The most efficient exchange of oxygen takes place in the bottom half of the lungs. The diaphragm is shaped rather like a parachute.

Emptying your lungs

Breathing out correctly can be likened to emptying your garbage bin to make room for more. You need to empty the whole bin before you start filling it up again. Likewise, you need to empty your lungs completely before you take in another breath.

During any type of exercise, once you have completely breathed out, avoid holding your breath. If you do not breathe in again, you take the risk of depriving the body of oxygen and a dangerous rise in blood pressure. Also, if you are not breathing properly, your performance would be unsatisfactory and you may feel unwell.

After training, slow, deep breathing and slow exhalation can help to relax the body.

Abdominal or diaphragmatic breathing

Practise this technique when you are resting and relaxed, then start to incorporate the technique into your workout sessions. You will soon be able to increase the intensity level of your training session and sustain it at a higher level for longer.

1 *Place one hand on your stomach and the other hand on your chest. As you breathe in, look at your hands. The hand on your stomach should be moving more than the hand on your chest. When this happens, you know you are making good use of the space at the bottom of your lungs.*

2 *Next, take a deep breath in through your nose and out slowly through your mouth. When you think you have breathed out fully, contract your stomach muscles to help empty your lungs completely. Breathing out should take twice as long as breathing in. Repeat this technique for 3 to 4 minutes at a time.*

Bellows breathing

Athletes often use this technique at the start of a competition because, by making the muscles involved in heavy breathing ready for action, it conditions the body to overcome the shock of a sudden demand for more oxygen. This method of breathing can help to combat fatigue, as it releases energizing chemicals to your brain.

1 *Sit in a chair the first time you attempt bellows breathing because it can cause hyperventilation, and in some cases people may pass out. When you are confident that you can use the technique safely, do it standing up, with your arms out to your side.*

2 *Breathe in fast through your nose and mouth, then breathe out fast through your mouth, using your abdominal muscles to empty your lungs completely. Try bellows breathing for 10 seconds, then increase by 5 seconds each time you practise the exercise.*

Levels of Intensity

Doing the same 30 minutes of cardiovascular exercise every day will not continue to give you the results you need. To prevent your body from getting used to any one style of exercise – and so making it ineffective – you need to vary your intensity levels.

To achieve dramatic results through cardiovascular training, you need to learn more about your training and apply levels of intensity to your training routine. Heart rate is perhaps the best measure of intensity because it indicates how hard your body is working. To get the best results from your exercise routine, follow the four levels of intensity.

Level 1: Steady, long-duration training

This lasts for at least 1 hour. Your heart rate should be between 40 and 60 per cent of maximum and you should be able to hold a normal conversation without effort or panting. If you are new to exercise, this is the level at which you will spend most of your time for the first few weeks. It is the least demanding, but it will start to promote an efficient cardiovascular system. If you are unfit, there is no point in trying to go above

Below: Level 1 is simply walking steadily for about one hour, while still being able to drink and eat.

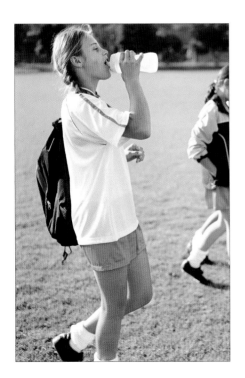

this level quickly, because you will tire too early to get a beneficial session. Walking fast for 40 minutes is far more beneficial than running for 5 minutes and being too tired to go any farther. Top athletes use this level of intensity to begin their warm-ups.

Level 2: Medium-intensity training

You should use this for 15 to 60 minutes of cardiovascular training. Your heart rate should be between 60 and 75 per cent of maximum – a rate at which you can only hold a conversation in short sentences. This level is great for weight loss and improving aerobic capacity without the risk of injury, but you have to make a conscious effort to stay at this level. (Aerobic capacity is the

Above: At Level 2, the pace is faster but still allows joggers to be able to speak comfortably.

highest amount of oxygen consumed during maximal exercise in activities that use the large muscle groups in the legs, or in the arms and legs combined.)

Fat burning myth

It is a myth that to burn fat you need to keep your heart rate low and keep going for a long period of time. In fact, the best way to lose fat is to adjust your intensity to challenge your body by making the exercise much harder, which in turn will burn more calories.

Pyramid of intensity

Imagine a pyramid where the base of the pyramid is Level 1. As you start to go up the pyramid, your level of intensity increases until you are training at Level 4, at the top. The base of the pyramid is wider indicating the amount of time you need to spend at this level of intensity to make your body efficient at coping with the demands of your exercise. If the pyramid has a narrow base, it will be more likely to topple over when you are at the top. This theory applies directly to your training. If you try to train at a high-intensity level without building a good base, you will be prone to injuries and overtraining.

Level 3: High-intensity training

This should last from 1 to 10 minutes, although trained athletes can continue at this level for longer due to their high aerobic capacity. Your heart rate should be between 75 and 90 per cent of maximum. You should only be able to give one-word answers during this type of training as you will be fully focused on breathing in as much oxygen as possible. Athletes often use this level of training in the form of intervals. For

Right: At Level 3, the going gets tougher, with the person running so hard that they start to get out of breath.

Below: The maximum level is Level 4, in which the runner pushes as hard as possible for a short sustained effort.

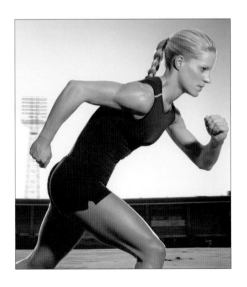

example, 10 minutes at Level 2, then 2 minutes at Level 3, then 2 minutes at Level 2, followed by 4 minutes at Level 3. This is often called Aerobic Interval Training. It is important to vary the duration of the intervals to achieve the best results. This is hard to begin with, but your body will adjust and be able to recover quickly between the intervals. This is the fastest way to develop muscle and increase your fat metabolism.

Level 4: Maximum-intensity training

This should last between 10 seconds and 2 minutes. This level is 90 per cent and above of maximum heart rate.

You will not be able to talk comfortably and you will feel out of breath from start to finish. As with Level 3, this level is used for interval training. For example, after 10 minutes' warm-up, walk for 1 minute, sprint as fast as possible for 30 seconds, then walk for 1 minute and, finally, sprint again for 30 seconds.

Sports people who play in positions that require the maximum amount of speed over short distances should adopt this type of intensity training. Do not, however, attempt to start this extreme type of training unless you have already been doing some reasonably intense training for some time.

Climate and Performance

Temperature, altitude, wind and humidity can all have significant effects on the body's ability to perform. It is absolutely essential that you understand these factors before attempting to train or compete in conditions that could have very serious adverse effects on your body.

One of the biggest factors that can affect your performance when training or competing in sports events is the prevailing temperature.

Your core body temperature is regulated at 37°C/98.6°F. If your body temperature changes by even just a few degrees above or below this level, you will become extremely unwell. Our natural reaction to combat overheating is to sweat. This creates a layer of water on the skin that helps to cool the body. Conversely, if we are too cold, we shiver, which increases muscle activity and in the process generates heat. We can, of course, also help to regulate our temperature by adding or removing layers of clothing.

Extreme heat

Exercising in the heat can be just as dangerous as exercising in low temperatures – and you should never attempt it without a full understanding of all the factors involved and being properly prepared. As soon as the air temperature rises above 32°C/89.6°F, you are entering the danger zone of heat cramps, heat exhaustion or even heatstroke. Heat cramps are similar to muscle cramps, and are caused by exertion and insufficient salts. Heat exhaustion is caused by a lack of the bodily fluids that would normally help cool you down. The signs of heat exhaustion are excessive sweating, pale skin, faster pulse and breathing rates, general weakness, nausea and vomiting. Heatstroke occurs when there is an increase in core body temperature due to a lack of fluids, or when the heat is so extreme that it overpowers your body's cooling mechanism. Too much water is lost via sweating and the volume of blood decreases so that there is less blood flow between the muscles and skin and less cooling, so that the body overheats. The

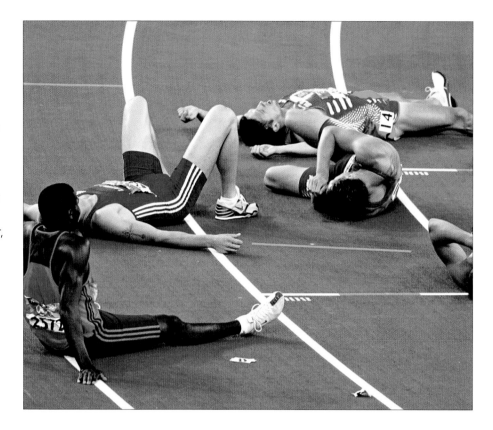

signs of heatstroke are the same as heat exhaustion, with possibly the additional symptom of dilated pupils. Heatstroke can be fatal. To avoid overheating, make sure you do not exercise in extreme temperatures, and avoid dangerous dehydration by drinking plenty of fluids before, during and after exercising. The amount you drink will depend on how hard you are exercising, your weight and the prevailing air temperature.

Wind

Weather conditions such as wind will either help or hinder your performance. For example, if you cycle with the wind

Above: Athletes at the Athens 2004 Olympics lie on the track suffering from heat exhaustion.

behind you, it will help you to go faster. If the wind is blowing toward you, it will slow you down. You should take this into consideration when you are trying to train at certain levels of intensity – there is no point in trying to beat a personal best time if you are cycling or running into a headwind.

Wind will take away the warm air close to your body and replace it with cooler air, lowering your body temperature in the process. The wind

Exercise and high temperatures	
Temperature – °C/°F	**Type of heat injury**
32–40/89.6–104	Heat cramps
40–54/104–129.2	Heat cramps, heat exhaustion, possibility of heatstroke
54/129.2+	Heatstroke very likely

chill factor is a scale that shows the equivalent temperature given to a particular wind speed. In hot conditions, wind will interfere with your body's natural cooling mechanism by drying the layer of sweat on your body that would normally cool you down.

Humidity

The ratio of water in the air at a particular temperature to the total quantity of moisture that could be carried in that air is defined as humidity. It is expressed as a percentage. If the level of humidity is high (30 per cent and above), you will sweat more, but the sweat cannot evaporate, hampering the body's ability to cool itself. This will lead to dehydration and the same problems associated with exercising in hot temperatures. To help overcome high humidity, drink fluids containing essential salts and minerals to keep your body functioning as normally as possible.

Below: When exercising in very cold weather, it is important to keep moving around and to wear adequate clothing.

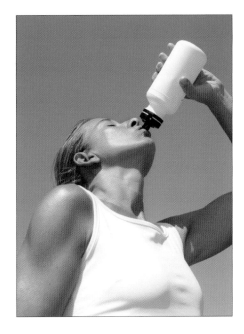

Above: In hot or humid conditions, drink plenty of liquids before, during and after your exercise programme.

Altitude

As altitude increases, atmospheric pressure drops and there is a decrease in the amount of oxygen available. Your maximal aerobic ability is reduced by

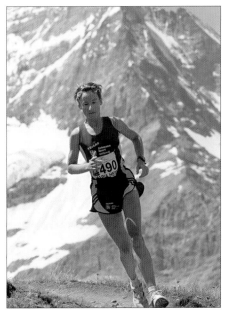

Above: If you run in the mountains, where there is an increase in altitude, you will need a few days to adapt.

1 per cent for every 91m/300ft above 1,372m/4,500ft. To exercise at high altitude, your body will have to go through short- and long-term adaptive changes. At first, you will experience a more rapid breathing rate and increased blood flow when exercising, and you will find yourself tiring very quickly. You may get acute mountain sickness, feelings of nausea, headaches, insomnia, dizziness and muscle weakness.

However, in just one or two days, your body will have adapted. Your resting heart rate will increase, as will your cardiac output (blood flow), in order to compensate for the lack of oxygen. After three to four weeks, your blood haemoglobin level will increase – every drop of blood that supplies the muscle will deliver an increased amount of oxygen. (Haemoglobin is a protein in the blood that contains iron and transports oxygen from the lungs to the rest of the body.)

If you live at high altitude for some time, your body will naturally adapt to the atmospheric conditions by producing more of the myoglobin, mitochondria and metabolic enzymes used for aerobic energy transfer.

However, you can also expect to lose muscle mass and body fat, which may affect your performance.

Walking

It's tempting to think that there's nothing to walking beyond putting one foot in front of the other and setting off. True, it is a very accessible form of exercise. However, getting the best from it calls for the right technique, pace, clothing and footwear – and a schedule.

Walking has many benefits. It's free, it's an independent mode of transport and environmentally friendly. It is also a great way to get fit before progressing to harder forms of exercise, such as running or preparing yourself for a bigger goal such as a marathon. Walking at a brisk pace will burn between 300 and 400 calories per hour and because walking has only one-third as much impact as running, it is an ideal form of exercise for people who suffer from bone-degenerating diseases such as osteoporosis.

Technique

Try to focus on a different aspect of your technique each time you walk. It is important to keep your head still with your chin parallel to the ground to eliminate using unnecessary energy. Stand tall when you walk, keep your abdominals and buttocks tensed to keep your spine in a good neutral position, and bend your elbows at 90 degrees. To make your walking workout even more demanding, carry dumbbells or

Below: Listening to the radio or music through headphones will keep you company while you are walking.

Above: Carrying dumbbells while walking very briskly gives you a much more vigorous workout.

hand weights. The key to walking more efficiently is to increase your stride rate and maintain flexibility in the hips. Your foot should strike the ground with your heel first, before rolling forward on to your toes.

What to wear

It is essential to have the right clothes and footwear for walking exercise. Make sure that you are properly fitted

Walking speed

The following chart will give you a guide to your walking speed. The next time you are walking for an exercise session, try counting the number of strides you take in 1 minute.

Steps per minute	kph	mph
70	3.2	2
90	4	2.5
105	4.8	3
120	5.6	3.5
140	6.4	4

Fast pace

In order to lose weight and change your body shape, you need to walk at a brisk pace of approximately 6.4kph/4mph. Wear loose clothing and comfortable shoes.

for your walking shoes. There should be a certain amount of comfort to begin with, but be aware that shoes will get more comfortable as the material softens and you wear them in. Therefore, you should buy shoes that are a half to a whole size too large so that you have room for your feet to expand when they get hot. If you are going to walk on the side of the road or on smooth walking tracks, you can wear normal running shoes. However, if you are going off-road, you will need a shoe with ankle support to protect your ankles from turning over on rough terrain. You should also wear several layers of clothing so that you can adjust them as necessary.

Below: Correct clothing and footwear suitable for the weather conditions and terrain are essential.

Walking exercises

Follow this six-week walking programme for four days a week, to improve your fitness. Although fast walking has less impact than running, equip yourself with comfortable walking shoes, and wear layers of clothing that you can peel off if you become overheated. The total walking time each week should increase week by week as you progressively get fitter and faster. If you are serious about stepping up your fitness, consider other aspects such as flexibility, core stability, strength and nutrition to get the desired results. After just six weeks of working through these exercises, you should be able to walk across hilly terrain for 60 minutes without stopping. Your recovery should be good enough for you to continue without taking any rests. To avoid dehydration, make sure you take fluids with you if you are out walking for more than 45 minutes.

Time	Intensity/environment
Week 1	
20 minutes	flat terrain
30 minutes	flat terrain, alternating 1 minute fast, 2 minutes slow
30 minutes	hilly terrain
20 minutes	flat or hilly terrain, with hand weights or a backpack

Weekly total: 1 hr 40 minutes

Time	Intensity/environment
Week 2	
25 minutes,	flat terrain
30 minutes	flat terrain, alternating 2 minutes fast, 2 minutes slow
35 minutes	hilly terrain
20 minutes	flat or hilly terrain, with hand weights or a backpack

Weekly total: 1 hr 50 minutes

Time	Intensity/environment
Week 3	
25 minutes	flat terrain
30 minutes	flat terrain, alternating 2 minutes fast, 2 minutes slow
40 minutes	hilly terrain
20 minutes	flat or hilly terrain, with hand weights or a backpack

Weekly total: 1 hr 55 minutes

Time	Intensity/environment
Week 4	
30 minutes	flat terrain
35 minutes	flat terrain, alternating 2 minutes fast, 1 minute slow
40 minutes	hilly terrain
20 minutes	flat or hilly terrain, with hand weights or a backpack

Weekly total: 2 hrs 5 minutes

Time	Intensity/environment
Week 5	
35 minutes	flat terrain
40 minutes	flat terrain, alternating 2 minutes fast, 1 minute slow
50 minutes	hilly terrain
25 minutes	flat or hilly terrain, with hand weights or a backpack

Weekly total: 2 hrs 30 minutes

Time	Intensity/environment
Week 6	
35 minutes	flat terrain
40 minutes	flat terrain, alternating 2 minutes fast, 1 minute slow
60 minutes	hilly terrain
25 minutes	flat or hilly terrain, with hand weights or a backpack

Weekly total: 2 hrs 40 minutes

Running

Like walking, running is a cheap form of exercise enjoyed by many people – though not everyone. Again, however, you don't just put your shoes on and go until you stop. Technique, stride, uphill and downhill terrain, and correct breathing are all important.

Running is one of the best forms of cardiovascular exercise as it doesn't require any expensive equipment and you can run just about anywhere.

Anyone can run, at any age. People have different motives for running: the initial reason may be to lose weight, then the person finds that they enjoy running and want to progress further in the sport, progressing until they can take part in races. For others, running is a simple form of exercise that can be done anytime, anywhere when convenient, and involves only the purchase of a good pair of running shoes and tracksuit.

Muscles used in running

The major muscles used in running are listed below. They are involved in driving you forward as well as taking the shock of the impact as your feet hit the ground. They also prevent injury and loss of energy caused by unnecessary movement.

The next step is technique. Good running technique is essential to enable you to run faster and avoid injury. As your foot strikes the ground, it should be in line with your hips and below your centre of gravity. Make sure that you have some flexion in your knee in the impact, and keep your hips stable to provide a strong base for driving forward.

Also, you need to be aware of lateral movement in the hips when you strike the ground, as this can lead to injuries. Do one-leg squats and superman exercises for the sides of the hips. To check for a weakness in the hip area,

gluteus maximus

biceps femoris

gastrocnemius

hip flexors

quadriceps

soleus

> ### Save energy
> If you are running long distances, avoid picking your legs up behind you too high. This could have the effect of causing lower back and pelvis injuries, and also wastes energy.

stand on one leg and squat down, trying to keep your hips from pushing out to the sides. Your waist line should be level throughout the squat.

After your foot strikes the ground, let your leg stretch fully behind you and at the same time drive your other leg forward to make contact with the ground. Throughout the running movement, keep your arms bent, but relaxed, at 90 degrees at the elbow. Your opposite hand should drive forward as your knee drives forward and upward. Don't let your lower back do all the work. It is a common mistake to twist the upper body from the lower back, rather than pumping the arms forward and back.

The importance of stride
Stride length and stride speed are both important. Generally, stride length will make you run faster, but this is not always the best way to gain speed. Do not try to lengthen your stride until your stride pace is sufficient. Most people make the mistake of overstriding: they have a stride rate of 70–80 strides per minute, when, in fact, the most efficient

> ### Run away weight
> Running can burn between 400 and 1,500 calories per hour, depending on the speed and the body mass of the individual runner. The faster you go and the heavier you are, the more calories you will burn.

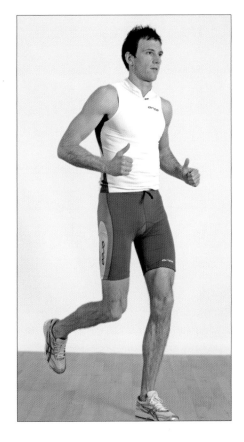

Above: When running, the foot should strike the ground in line with your hips and below your centre of gravity.

Above: When running faster, the opposite leg to the arm drives forward. The momentum helps to increase speed.

Above: For smooth, injury-free running, try to avoid lateral movement in the hips, and keep the legs moving forward.

stride rate is approximately 90 strides per minute. Next time you run, keep a count of your strides – if you are running at less than 90 strides per minute, try shortening your stride slightly and increasing your stride rate. Don't be put off if you find you cannot manage to change your stride at once. It could take a month or two before you naturally run at the higher stride rate.

Uphill and downhill

When you run uphill, try to keep the stride rate high. Shorten your stride to avoid early fatigue and overstretching the muscles in the back of the legs. Use your arms more – a sprinter gets around one-third of propulsion from the arms. When you are running downhill, try to keep your stride length short and fast, in order to avoid injuring your legs – as a greater stride length creates more impact and increases the chances of injury.

Right: One-leg squats, which can be done in the gym, exercise the same muscles involved in running.

Breathing

To complete the correct technique, your breathing has to be right. There are a number of ways to try to breathe when you are running. Most runners use a 2:2

technique, that is, two strides on each leg (a total of four strides) to every time you breathe in, and two strides to every time you breathe out. You can use a 3:3 or even 4:4 technique, if you prefer.

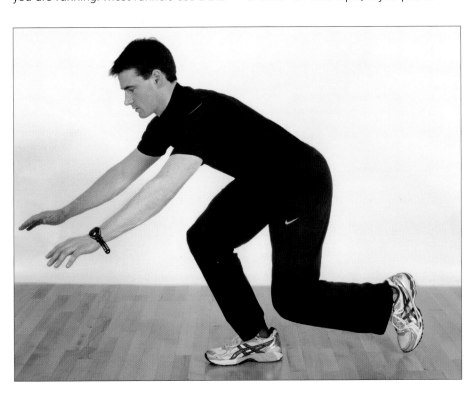

Cycling

Although not as cheap as walking or running, cycling is a relatively inexpensive and highly enjoyable way to keep fit, lose weight and enjoy the great outdoors. As ever, good technique, proper kit and an effective schedule will pay fitness dividends.

Cycling is an excellent form of low-impact aerobic exercise that burns up calories. Calorie burn ranges from 150 calories per hour for a small person travelling at 8kph/5mph to over 800 calories per hour for a bigger person travelling uphill or at over 32kph/20mph.

Technique

If the saddle on your bike is too low, you won't be able to make full use of the power in your legs. If the saddle is too high, you will feel your hips roll from side to side as your legs are stretched too far at the bottom of each pedal stroke. To get the saddle height correct, sit on the bike with one of the pedals at 6 o'clock. In this position, your leg should be almost straight.

To adjust the fore and aft position of the saddle, put one of the crank arms at 3 o'clock. The front of your knee should be in vertical line with the axle of the pedal. If the saddle is too far back or forward, you will put too much pressure on your knees and be at risk of injury.

If the handlebars are too low, you will get backache, so make sure the bars are not much lower than your hips. Put the

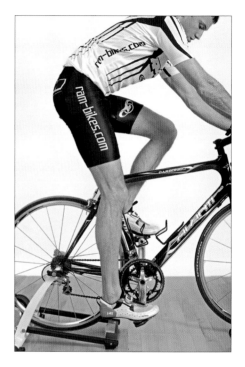

Above: When the saddle is the correct height, your leg should be almost straight in the 6 o'clock position.

bars higher than this for added comfort. The distance between the saddle and bars is also important. Make sure you can reach the bars with arms still slightly bent. If they are too close, your back will not be in the neutral position and will become rounded. If they are too far away, you will have to work your core muscles to stay in the right position, and this may result in lower back pain. Check constantly to make sure your neck and shoulders are relaxed to prevent unnecessary aches or pains.

To get the most efficient pedal stroke, pedal in circles rather than squares. In other words, use the whole of the pedal stroke to generate power rather than just pushing down from the top to the bottom. Pulling the pedal back up on the recovery part of the pedal stroke will give your hamstrings a good workout. As you reach the bottom of the pedal

Muscles used in cycling

The major muscles used in cycling are listed below. They are used to push the pedals down and pull them back up in a circular movement. Other muscles help to maintain stability and position on the bike.

hip flexors

gluteus maximus

quadriceps

biceps femoris

gastrocnemius

triceps

Cycling exercises

The following four cycling sessions are suitable for people at any level from beginner, through intermediate to expert. Just be realistic and make the appropriate choice for you, depending on whether your fitness level is below average, average or above average. Do not stick to your usual route. Instead, use these sessions to improve your training fitness and performance. Try to do cycling exercises three to four times a week using the sessions that match your fitness level. Always cool down at the end of your workout with about 5 minutes of easy pedalling as well as some stretches.

	Fitness level	Distance/time	Intensity
Session: time trials to monitor your progress	Below average:	5km/3.1 miles	fast as possible L3
	Average:	8km/5 miles	fast as possible L3
	Above average:	16km/10 miles	fast as possible L3–L4
Session 2: interval exercise to increase aerobic capacity and fitness time	Below average:	4 x 2 minutes	L3–L4 with 4 minutes easy L1 between efforts
	Average:	6 x 3 minutes	L3–L4 with 4 minutes easy L1 between efforts
	Above average:	6 x 4 minutes	L3–L4 with 3 minutes easy L1 between efforts
Session 3: sprints to improve anaerobic ability, recovery and leg speed. Revolutions per minute above 100 for the sprints	Below average:	20 minutes	L2 with 20-second sprints L4 every 4 minutes
	Average:	40 minutes	L2 with 30-second sprints L4 every 4 minutes
	Above average:	60 minutes	L2 with 30-second sprints L4 every 3 minutes
Session 4: hill exercises for leg strength and aerobic capacity. Use a harder gear and drop revs to 60–70 per minute.	Below average:	4 x 2 minute hills	L3 with 4 minutes on flat, L1 between hills
	Average:	6 x 3 minute hills	L3 with 3 minutes on flat, L1 between hills
	Above average:	6 x 4 minute hills	L3–L4 with 3 minutes on flat L1 between hills

stroke, push your heel down to get the full range of movement and make use of all the muscles at the front and back of your legs.

Below: For comfort, bend arms slightly at the elbow. To prevent soreness, keep your shoulders and neck relaxed.

The optimum pedal stroke rate is around 90–100rpm, which keeps you on top of the resistance and helps you to get the oxygen supply that is essential for your legs. Hard gears lower your pedal stroke rate and can cause you to build up lactic acid in your muscles, which may impair muscle contraction and cause a very unpleasant burning sensation.

Keep your upper body as relaxed as possible. Apart from pulling on the bars when you are going up a steep hill, try to conserve your energy and have a more comfortable ride by working your legs and consciously keeping your grip, neck and shoulders as relaxed as you can.

Getting started

If you want to use cycling for improved cardiovascular fitness, incorporate the sessions above into your training plan. Warm up with 5 to 10 minutes' easy pedalling that gradually becomes harder, followed by light stretches for your lower back, hamstrings, quadriceps and calves.

What to wear

A well-fitting helmet is essential – it could save your life if you are involved in an accident. Wear gloves to help you grip the handlebars and avoid sores and blisters. Your footwear will vary depending on your level of cycling. The most efficient shoes have stiff soles so that you can get maximum power through the pedals. Wear cycling shorts to give you protection and comfort.

Exercise bike versus outdoors

For anyone who prefers a more controlled environment, an exercise bike offers simulated hills and flats, and allows you to monitor your heart rate while you are exercising. Using an exercise bike requires little co-ordination and there is less strain on the ankle, knee and hip joints, especially for beginners, anyone elderly or people who are recovering from injuries.

However, if you like being outdoors, enjoy looking at the scenery and experiencing different terrains, riding a dynamic bicycle is a great way to get fit.

Cross-trainer

The cross-trainer is a highly effective, all-over body exercise that uses a large number of muscles. It offers a great alternative to running and is an excellent way to exercise for people who suffer from back and joint problems.

The cross-trainer is a low-impact alternative that works the same muscles that you use when running, but without the same physical impact of pounding the floor. The action of pushing and pulling with the arms simulates the action of cross-country skiing and hill-walking with poles. It also gives you great upper-body tone. If you are looking to do an all-over body weight-training session, the cross-trainer will provide you with a great warm-up.

Technique

Before you begin exercising on the cross-trainer, check to see if you are in the right position. If your feet are too far apart, your stride may force you to overstretch, which could cause an injury. Adjust the step length until you feel comfortable. Keep your posture upright

Below: Unlike running, the cross-trainer works all the major muscle groups in the body.

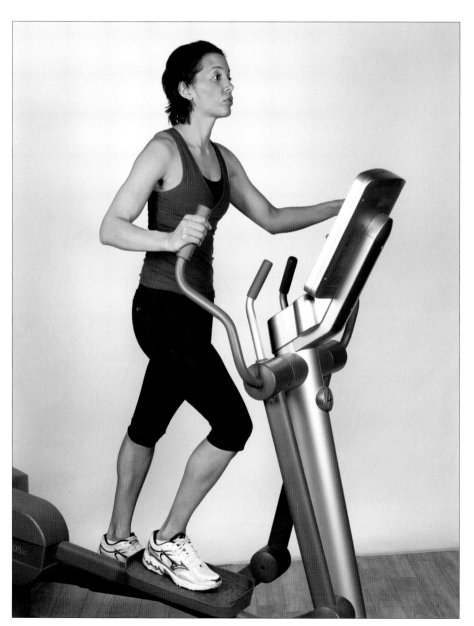

> **Target problem areas**
>
> Change the emphasis of your workout according to the body parts that you want to work hardest. For example, if you want to work your arms, then relax your legs and just let them follow as you drive the machine with your arms. Conversely, relax the arms so you can work the legs.

– your back should be straight, your shoulders back, chin up and your core muscles, especially abdominals, switched on to work hard. Try not to let your arms do too much of the work. Instead, really use your legs to drive the machine forward. When your leg drives the foot plate back, ensure that the back of your leg is fully extended to have maximum effect on the muscles at the back of your leg.

Avoid wearing training shoes that have too much grip. Your feet need to be able to move slightly in the shoes to find their natural position as you push down on the footplates.

To make the best use of your legs, resist bending forward when you start to feel fatigued. Bending forward will force your lower back to provide the power to drive the machine, and it will quickly tire. If this happens for long periods of time, you may be at risk of a lower-back overuse injury.

> **Warning**
>
> If you suffer from hip and lower back problems, do not at first spend too much time on the cross-trainer. Start with a maximum of around 10 minutes and gradually build it up, by around 3 to 5 minutes every session, until you are comfortable exercising for about 30 minutes.

Above: This position is too far back on the cross-trainer to have any significant effect on the muscles.

Above: The ideal position is a straight back, shoulders back and chin up. Let your legs do all the work.

Above: Leaning too far forward will cause strain on the arms and the back and neck will feel uncomfortable.

Getting started

Each cross-trainer will have different resistance or gradient settings. You should adjust these settings depending on your fitness level and weight. Your level should be adjusted depending on the type of training session that you want to do: long and steady to train your endurance; or fast, powerful intervals to increase your aerobic threshold. Rhythm is the key. You should feel as if you are keeping up with the machine or, ideally, you should stay slightly ahead of the machine, rather than losing rhythm and feeling as if you are struggling. To set your training levels, follow the principles relating to levels of intensity set out earlier in the book.

Post injury

If you are recovering from a running injury, use the cross-trainer to do similar training, but without the same physical impact on your joints and muscles, especially after Achilles tendon, feet, knee, pelvic and lower-back injuries.

Cross-trainer exercises

Include the following training sessions in your weekly programme to get the most out of this type of cardiovascular exercise. Check that you are in the correct position on the cross-trainer. Before you begin any of the sessions, make sure you do at least 5 minutes' warm-up at Level 1 intensity, including some stretches for the lower back, quadriceps, hamstrings and calves.

	Fitness level	Distance/time	Intensity
Session 1: aerobic endurance	Below average:	20 minutes	L2 continuous
	Average:	40 minutes	L2 continuous
	Above average:	60 minutes	L2 continuous
Session 2: improved fitness and aerobic capacity	Below average:	4 x 3 minutes	L3 with 3 minutes L1 easy between efforts
	Average:	5 x 4 minutes	L3 with 3 minutes L1 easy between efforts
	Above average:	6 x 4 minutes	L3–L4 with 3 minutes L1 easy between efforts
Session 3: a new level of fitness, and anaerobic workout	Below average:	20 minutes	L2 with 20-second sprints L4 every 4 minutes
	Average:	40 minutes	L2 with 30-second sprints L4 every 3 minutes
	Above average:	60 minutes	L2 with 30-second sprints L4 every 3 minutes

Rowing

Few cardiovascular exercises use the upper body to the same extent that rowing does. Rowing burns 600–1,000 calories per hour, making it one of the most effective exercises for burning calories and losing weight.

As well as giving you an excellent cardiovascular workout, rowing also exercises all the major muscles.

Technique

Hold the handle in front of you, arms straight and in line with the rowing chain. Your body should be curled up toward the front of the machine like a coiled spring. Initiate the pull by driving your legs as if you are doing a leg press. Take your arms with you as you straighten your legs. As your legs straighten, pull the handle in toward your lower chest and abdomen. Pause for 1 second – the recovery phase – then straighten your arms and bring your legs back to the coil position. Take your time in the recovery phase. Check your stroke rate, which will change depending on whether you are doing speed-work intervals or long-distance endurance. Aim for 25–35 strokes per minute. Your breathing needs to be correct, because the large number of muscles used in rowing demand a lot of oxygen. Breathe in as you recover into the coil, and out as you explode back in the pull.

Muscles exercised during rowing

Most of the muscles in your body are used for rowing; the picture below shows the major muscles working. Rowing regularly is a good cardiovascular exercise that is ideal for strengthening your shoulder, arm, abdomen and back muscles.

lattissimus dorsi

quadriceps

biceps

rhomboids

biceps femoris

Rowing exercises

Include the following training sessions in your weekly programme to get the most from this cardiovascular exercise. Before any of the sessions, make sure you do at least 5 minutes' warm-up at Level 1 intensity, and because rowing strengthens all the main muscles, it is best to warm them up first with some stretches for the lower back, quadriceps, hamstrings and calves.

	Fitness level	Distance/time	Intensity
Session 1: time trials to help monitor your fitness	Below average:	1km/0.6 miles	L2–L3
	Average:	2km/1.2 miles	L2–L3
	Above average:	2km/1.2 miles	L2–L3
Session 2: improving fitness level and aerobic capacity	Below average:	4 x 200m/219yd	intervals with 60 seconds' rest between each one L3
	Average:	8 x 200m/219yd	intervals with 45 seconds' rest between each one L3
	Above average:	16 x 200m/219yd	intervals with 30 seconds' rest between each one L3
Session 3: improving rowing efficiency and burning calories for weight loss and maintenance	Below average:	2km/1.2 miles	long-distance, steady row L2
	Average:	5km/3.1 miles	long-distance row L2
	Above average:	1km/0.6 miles	long-distance row L2

Above: Before starting your rowing exercises, the body is set in a coiled spring position.

Above: Drive the machine back with the legs, pulling the arms back with you as you begin to straighten your legs.

Above: As the legs are extended, pull your arms toward your lower chest and abdomen.

There are a number of technique faults that you should look out for and correct in order to prevent injury and make your rowing more energy-efficient.

Common faults

• Leaning forward as you go into the coil position: keep the back straight and bend your legs more in the coil position so that you don't have to lean forward to get a long stroke.
• Bent arms in the pull phase: correct bent arms by using your legs more. Your legs are approximately five times stronger than your arms, so keep your arms straight until your legs are almost straight, and your legs will do most of the work.
• Leaning back too much at the end of the stroke: leaning back will give you a

longer pull but can cause lower back injuries. Try to keep your back as upright as possible until you have the core strength to allow you to lean back slightly.
• Grip too tight: a tight grip is fine for short, fast-interval sessions because you get a chance to put the handle down and relax between efforts. However, for longer distances, such as those over 1km/1,094yd, you need to keep your grip relaxed in order to prevent your forearms from getting too tight and cramping. If you are rowing long distances, try changing the position of your thumb. Instead of wrapping it under the handle, rest it on top to use different hand muscles.

Getting started

If you are using the rowing machine for the first time, start with the below-average fitness sessions (*see* Rowing exercises). After six weeks, move up to the average fitness sessions. Wait at least another six weeks before you attempt the above-average fitness stage. Before you do any of these sessions, start with a 500m/547yd warm-up at Level 1, followed by back, arm and leg stretches.

Set your target

Professional rowers are able to row 2km/1.2 miles in less than 6 minutes. If you are starting out, 8 minutes is a good target to try to achieve for this distance.

Below: Leaning too far forward means that you have to expend far more energy to drive back.

Below: Wait for the legs to be fully extended before pulling the arms in toward your chest.

Below: Leaning back too much at the end of the stroke can cause injury to your lower back.

Swimming

For many people, swimming is simply an enjoyable bit of splashing about at the pool or the seaside. Beyond that, though, it can improve your cardiovascular fitness as well as muscular strength without any impact, because it is non-weight bearing.

There are a number of different swimming strokes you can use, which use different muscles. Try to use a combination of strokes to ensure that all your muscles are worked.

Freestyle

Front crawl is usually now referred to as freestyle. The arms are mainly used to get the forward motion, with the legs producing only 10 per cent of the forward energy. However, your legs do play a vital role in keeping your body balanced and in preventing excess drag. Keep your hand slightly cupped as it enters the water and reaches forward

Muscles used in swimming

These are the main muscles used in swimming. Each stroke will place different demands and movement patterns on the muscles. Using these muscles in conjunction with correct technique will improve your swimming.

- triceps
- biceps
- latissimus dorsi
- hip flexor
- gluteus
- rectus femoris

Above: Take a breath as your arm and head come out of the water and before your hand re-enters the water.

and outward to catch the water. Sweep your hand outward and press the water laterally to your body, then sweep your hand in toward your hips. To finish the stroke, press the water down toward your hips, extending your arm as much as possible. On recovery to the next stroke, your elbow leaves the water first. You then reach forward, keeping your elbow high so that you don't slap the water as your hand re-enters it. Keep kicking with your legs at all times.
Tip At mid-stroke, slightly dropping the shoulder of your arm under the water will promote a better stroke and help the opposite arm to recover.

Butterfly

The butterfly is one of the hardest to perfect. The timing of the arm pull and leg kick is essential for a continuous efficient stroke. Your fingers should enter the water first, just as your legs finish their big kick. At this point, your arms should begin to bend as they press laterally, and the small leg kick begins. You then turn your hands and press them toward your body as the small leg kick finishes. You finish the stroke by pushing your hands toward your feet with straight arms, followed by the

Above: For the butterfly, as you reach forward for the next stroke, your upper body comes up out of the water.

quick exit of the hands from the water and the start of the big leg kick as your arms recover and reach forward to re-enter the water.
Tip Arch your lower back as you do the big kick so that you can help to get your upper body reaching forward for the next stroke.

Backstroke

Your legs are vital in the backstroke and should be kicking all the time below the surface of the water for maximum efficiency. Your little finger

Below: In the backstroke, the arms supply forward movement. One arm is in recovery while the other is in the water.

Swimming exercises

If you include the following three sessions as part of your main set of exercises, you will get fitter and faster in the water. Keep a diary of your times and comments to help monitor your improved performance. For the cool-down after you have done the main set of three sessions, choose any stroke you prefer and carry out at least 100m/109yd of easy swimming, focusing on breathing and trying to remain relaxed.

	Fitness level	Distance/time	Intensity
Session 1: time trials to help monitor your fitness	Below average:	10 minutes' continuous	go as far as you can L2–L3
	Average:	800m/875yd continuous	L2–L3 and note the time
	Above average:	1,500m/1,640yd continuous	L2–L3 and note the time
Session 2: improved fitness level and aerobic capacity	Below average:	8 x 25m/27yd intervals	with 60 seconds' rest between each one L3–L4
	Average:	10 x 50m/55yd intervals	with 30 seconds' recovery between each one L3–L4
	Above average:	10 x 100m/109yd intervals	with 30 seconds' recovery between each one L3–L4
Session 3: improved endurance	Below average:	20 minutes	L2
	Average:	40 minutes	L2
	Above average:	90 minutes	L2

---

should enter the water first, then your whole arm, with hand cupped to catch the water. Flex your elbow and press the water laterally, then downward, until your hand is just about level with your chest. To finish the stroke, press your hand down toward your feet, keeping it close to your body. When your arm is fully straightened, start the recovery by taking your thumb out of the water first and rotating your shoulder joint, allowing your little finger to enter the water first on re-entry.

Tip Keep your head as flat as possible, with eyes looking up to the ceiling, to minimize drag in the water.

Below: An efficient breathing technique is crucial for a good performance in strokes such as the butterfly.

Breaststroke

For an effective breaststroke, it is essential to get the timing of your legs and arms right in order to cover the maximum distance with the least amount of effort. Start by pushing your arms out in front of you to create a forward glide as your legs kick back. Cup the water and press your hands against the water laterally, arms slightly bent, then sweep your hands in toward your chest and start the upward leg movement in preparation for the kick. To complete the stroke, thrust your hands forward to the straight-arm position as the leg kick starts.

Breathing

When you are swimming, breathing correctly takes practice. You should decide which method of breathing works best for you: trickle breathing or explosive breathing. Trickle breathing involves slowly breathing out when your head is down in the water, and then taking a breath in on the recovery as your head comes out of the water. Explosive breathing requires you to hold your breath while your head is in the water, then quickly breathing out and back in as you lift your head out of the water in the recovery.

Warning

Breaststroke can be bad for you if you have a weak lower back, hips or knees, as it involves a strong kicking action in an awkward position.

Getting started

A good swim session should be structured as follows: a good warm-up, main set and cool-down. Doing the technique drills before the main set will remind you what the correct technique should feel like. Before you start, warm-up with 5 minutes of easy swimming.

Below: Good aerodynamic technique is essential to cut through the water in backstroke.

Boxercise

Tense, stressful day at the office? Boxercise is just what you need to work it out of your system. And you don't have to get into the ring to enjoy the benefits of this popular sport. Many sports centres now run boxing-based exercise classes.

Boxercise is a sport that will improve your endurance, speed, power and core stability. It will also strengthen and tone your arms, legs and abdominals. The satisfaction of landing a correct punch will help to alleviate the stress induced by a long day pounding a keyboard or sitting through yet another meeting. It is also a great way to burn up to 500 calories per hour, so it's time to get the gloves on.

Technique

To get the correct stance, stand with your feet just over shoulder-width apart, with one foot slightly in front of the

Muscles used in boxing

pectorals

triceps

rhomboids
(middle to upper
back)

rectus
abdominis

obliques

The muscles illustrated represent those that are mainly used in boxercise. Some muscles will be used to make the punch while other muscles stabilize the rest of the body making the punch even more powerful.

Above: The correct stance when you are ready to attack is feet balanced, with hands raised to protect the face.

other. If you are right-handed, place your right foot slightly behind the line of the left foot, and vice versa if you are left-handed. If you are right-handed, your left hand should be in front. If you are left-handed, your right hand should be in front.

Getting started

Warm up with 5 to 10 minutes of cardiovascular exercise, such as running or rowing, and some light stretches and core exercises to prepare your muscles. You will need a pair of boxing gloves for yourself and pads for your training partner. To avoid injuries, your partner should, ideally, be someone of a similar size to you.

Begin by learning the three different punches – jab, hook and uppercut. Once you have mastered these, slowly build

up combinations to try to make it an exciting workout. Next, you can add some leg exercises, such as squats, lunges and side lunges as you do the boxing combinations to raise the heart rate further and make your legs work harder.

It is important to remember that this is not a contest to see who can hit the hardest. It is, instead, a good way to increase your heart rate to improve your fitness levels and burn calories. To get the most from your muscles, focus on mastering the technique, then you can go on to add speed and power.

Below: When sparring, always hit across at your partner's opposite hand.

Jab

Though not a particularly hard punch, the jab can be made more powerful by stepping into the punch with a short forward step. To maintain a high heart rate, use the jab more frequently than any other punch.

Watchpoint It is important to control your breathing, especially with long combinations of punches. Experiment to find the best breathing method for you. Try breathing out as you land every third punch, and in before the fourth punch.

1 *Stand with your feet shoulder-width apart, holding both hands up in front of your face to act as a guard. Your training partner holds the pads out in front of him, at your eye height, his arms slightly bent to absorb the punch.*

2 *With your right arm almost fully extended, throw a quick punch, straight and forward, to make contact with your partner's right pad. Your hand should finish in a horizontal position, the back of your hand facing upward.*

Hook

Aim to get a good follow through with this punch. Use your abdominal muscles to produce a powerful rotation of the body to add extra weight to the punch, and keep them tight to control the follow-through. If your follow-through is too big, you will risk overstretching other muscles, which can cause lower-back problems.

Watchpoint To help prevent wrist injuries, keep your wrists, elbows and shoulders in line at the same height for the jab and the hook punches.

 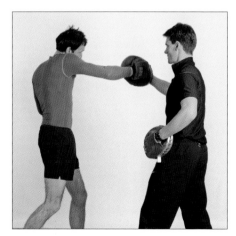

1 *Hold a hand up in front of your face to act as a guard. Your training partner holds the pads out to the side with his palms (face of the pad) facing in toward each other.*

2 *Take your right arm back round to the side of your body and then throw it back around in a semicircle to hit your partner's right pad, with your knuckles pointing forward.*

Uppercut

This is a powerful punch. Due to starting in a lower squatting position, you will use more muscle mass and momentum, so your partner should expect a big impact. Hit upward hard to raise your partner's hand.

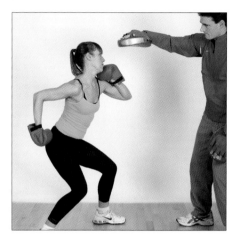

1 *Hold a hand up in front of your face to act as a guard. Squat down slightly by bending both knees. Your training partner stands close to you with the face of the pads facing the floor. Keep your balance throughout the movement.*

2 *From a bent-arm position, straighten your arms as you straighten your legs, and throw the punch up toward your partner's right pad. Make contact with your knuckles facing away from you.*

Combination punches

Experiment with different combinations of punches. For example, try two jabs with the left hand and then a hook with the right. Having mastered that, try four jabs then a squat, four hooks, a lunge, four uppercuts and a side lunge.

FLEXIBILITY AND INJURIES

Pre-exercise and post-exercise stretches are essential to avoid exercise-related injuries, to keep your muscles long and relaxed after training, and to allow them to recover for your next training session. This chapter combines flexibility exercises for all parts of the body with a self-help guide to common training injuries. It is not, however, a substitute for medical advice. When injured, always see a doctor. Include a variety of flexibility exercises in your routine to stretch your muscles from different angles.

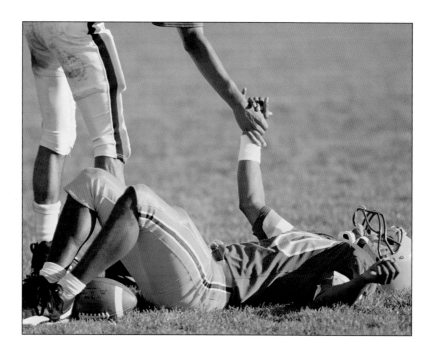

Above: Even with the maximum body protection, some sports are liable to cause more injury.
Left: Injuries can occur at any time and any place.

The Importance of Flexibility

Flexibility training is one of the most frequently ignored and least understood areas of most fitness routines. You should, however, treat it with all the seriousness and commitment that you would accord any other part of your training routine.

There are a number of reasons why flexibility is essential. If, to give one example, your calf muscles are tight before you start a 10km/6.2-mile race or training session, then you are far more likely to suffer from cramps and muscle tears. If you play contact sports, such as American football or rugby, and you go hard into a tackle, your neck may be vulnerable if you don't have a good range of movement – a stiff neck will put the muscles and tendons under significant pressure.

If you are a swimmer with limited mobility around the shoulder joint, the result will be poor technique, a weak performance and likelihood of injury.

Stretching to remain flexible is not a new concept for your body. Everyone is born with great flexibility but as we get older we become less and less flexible due to lack of activity, sitting for long periods of time, and injuries from everyday life and sport. Everyone needs to be flexible.

What is flexibility?

You may often hear the word 'flexibility' used in relation to fitness training, but what is it? It is the range of mobility around a joint and the muscles that surround it. Flexibility training should: reduce the risk of injury; create a good range of movement (especially as a muscle reaches its outer limits of movement); improve the movement around a joint; reduce muscular ache; increase co-ordination; increase blood flow circulation; break down scar tissue from general and overuse injuries; and equip the body to cope with the demands of a specific type of training or sport.

Sit and reach

The most commonly used test of flexibility is the sit and reach test. Thanks to the ample amount of research that has been carried out on the subject, it is fairly easy to compare yourself with other people. As a test, it illustrates the level of flexibility in your hamstrings and lower back. Studies show that there is direct correlation between flexibility in the hamstrings and the lower back, with muscular pain in the lower back, gait limitation and the risk of falling in older adults. (American College of Sports Medicine 1998.)

Use a sit and reach test box or simply make your own using a box and a solid ruler. Place the soles of your feet up

Left: The sit and reach test assesses the flexibility of the back and the hamstrings, at the back of the thigh.

Below left: To keep muscle flexibility during your training, stop now and again to do some stretches.

Sit and reach test

This simple test is a reliable measure of the flexibility of the hamstrings and the lower back.

	Male	**Female**
Very poor	−20cm/−7¾in	−15cm/−6in
Poor	−19 to 9cm/−7½ to 3½in	−14 to 8cm/−5½ to 3in
Fair	−8 to 1cm/−3 to ⅓in	−7 to 0cm/−2¾ to 0in
Average	0 to 5cm/0 to 2in	1 to 10cm/⅓ to 4in
Good	6 to 16cm/2⅓ to 6¼in	11 to 20cm/4⅓ to 7¾in
Excellent	17 to 27cm/6⅔ to 10½in	21 to 30cm/8¼ to 12in
Superior	27cm+/10½in+	30cm+/12in+

against the box and then, with your arms out in front of you and your legs straight, slowly reach forward along the ruler. After three attempts at stretching forward, you should be at your farthest point. The point where your fingers touch the ruler or box is your score (if you don't make it beyond your toes, you receive a negative score). The ruler should read zero where the soles of your feet are in contact with the box. Compare your score with the data in the box to see how flexible you are. Be aware that warm-up will make a massive difference to your flexibility, so always use the same warm-up before you do the test. About 5 minutes of cardiovascular exercise would be suitable.

When to stretch

You should try to stretch before and after every training session or competition. Before you begin any activity, warm up

Below: After you have completed your training programme, do some stretches to aid recovery.

first with some cardiovascular exercise to promote blood flow and heat in the muscles. For example, if you intend going for a 10km/6-mile run, do 5 minutes' fast walking. Follow this with 5 minutes of stretches, paying particular attention to your hamstrings, quadriceps and calf muscles. After the run, do static stretches in your cool-down. If you are intending to lift heavy weights, do 5 minutes' easy warm-up on the

Below: Stretching is beneficial to everyone, whatever their level of fitness or their age.

Above: When you begin any major training, always include stretches in your warm-up.

rowing machine before you do dynamic or proprioceptive muscular facilitation stretches (PMF stretching), paying particular attention to the muscle regions you may use. For example, before a chest weights session, stretch the pectorals, triceps and lower back. After the weights session, do static stretches to help lengthen the muscles back to full movement and decrease the risk of injury.

Types of Flexibility

The different types of stretching that should be included in you training programme are static active stretching, static passive stretching, ballistic stretching, isometric stretching and proprioceptive muscular facilitation.

Everyone wants to achieve greater flexibility in the shortest time possible, with minimum pain and risk, so that they can get on with their fitness training programme. The good news is that you can – and you don't need to get yourself into bizarre contortions as if you were auditioning for the circus in order to do so.

There are a number of different types of stretches that are suitable for inclusion in your training programme. First, though, you need to understand how the following types of stretches can help you, when it is appropriate to do them, and what exactly is meant by terms such as 'static active stretching', 'static passive stretching', 'dynamic stretching', 'ballistic stretching', 'isometric stretching' and 'proprioceptive muscular facilitation stretching' (PMF stretching).

When deciding which technique to use, think about the range of movement you are trying to achieve, and always use a variety of stretches to improve your flexibility. It is important to remember that stretching should not be painful. Simply getting into the correct stretching position and starting to feel the tension in the right muscle is enough. Some types of stretching are more aggressive than others, for example dynamic stretching or ballistic stretching. Before you do any of these types of stretches, make sure you warm up for at least 10–15 minutes in order to get adequate blood flow and heat in the muscles.

When not to stretch?

In some situations it may be best not to do any stretches. If you feel any discomfort in the muscle from an injury, leave the injury for at least 48 hours and consult a physician to determine whether it is safe to begin stretching the muscle. Avoid stretching areas that are suffering from muscular and ligament strains or areas of recent fractures. If you are at all unsure, get expert advice.

Static active stretching

This is a method of stretching muscles with minimal movement. An example would be placing one leg on a step and holding it there for 30 seconds. This is the best form of stretching for a cool-down after your training to help re-align the muscles and promote good blood flow. This type of stretch uses the opposing muscles to hold the stretch.

Static passive stretching

This stretch will increase the range of movement of a muscle. Unlike static active stretching, you will need to use an external force to stretch the muscle. Static passive stretching is best used after training or competition to realign the muscle fibres. It is often used for the rehabilitation of torn muscles.

> **Build in flexibility**
> To get the most out of exercise, it is important to get an understanding of which stretches and types of flexibility are going to be good for you.
>
> Flexibility is as necessary as any other training. Without a good programme of flexibility exercises, you will be more prone to injury. Injuries mean less training, or even no training as a result. So there are no excuses – make flexibility a vital part of your fitness training programme.

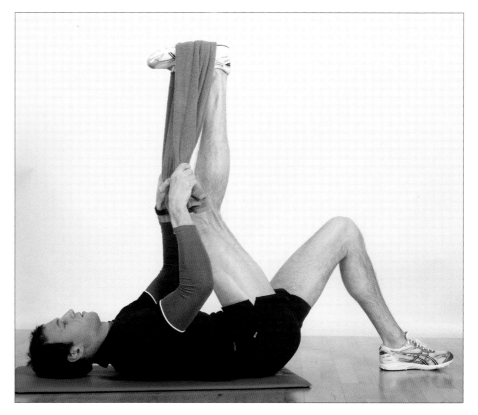

Hold a towel around your foot to pull it up by stretching your hamstrings. Hold the stretch for 20 to 30 seconds.

Dynamic stretching

This is a good way to warm up – but not after injury, as it could cause further damage. It uses training movements, such as lunges and squats, to warm up and stretch the muscles you will use in the activity. Your body's movement and momentum create the stretch. Ensure that your heart rate has been elevated for at least 10 minutes for sufficient blood flow and heat in the muscles.

This lunge with rotation has some momentum to get a good dynamic stretch. Maintaining your balance while stretching is important.

Isometric stretching

This uses the contraction of the muscle to stretch muscle fibres that are not being stretched in a normal passive stretch. Following the stretch, allow the quadriceps to contract for 3 to 5 seconds to wake up any fibres that are not being stretched. This creates a greater stretch response in the muscle fibres. When a muscle is contracted during exercise, not all the fibres are contracting; some are at rest. When a muscle is being stretched, some muscle fibres are elongated and some are not. During an isometric contraction, the muscle fibres will be pulled from both ends by the contracting muscles, so the resting fibres are stretched.

Lie on your front and have your training partner bend your leg up behind you to stretch your quadriceps muscles.

Proprioceptive muscular facilitation (PMF) stretching

This is commonly used in sports that require a larger range of movement, such as ballet and gymnastics. It involves a muscle being stretched by a partner. It is perhaps one of the most advanced forms of stretching and can often promote the best results. When contracting the muscles being stretched, do so for only 5 to 6 seconds, then stretch again for 10 seconds.

Have your training partner stretch your hamstrings until they reach stretching point. Resist by contracting your hamstrings to try to force your partner's arm back.

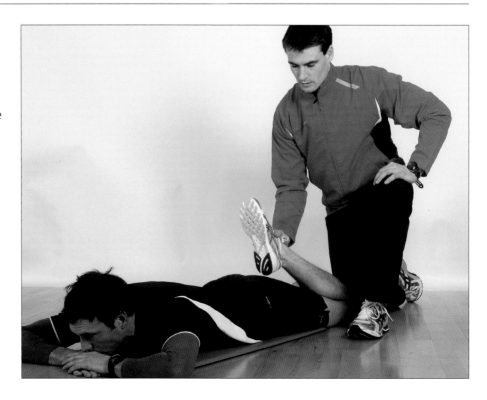

Shoulders

The shoulder joint has many moving parts, with muscles pulling from every direction, making it susceptible to injury. Because it has a large range of motion, and tends to be unstable, tears and inflammation can easily occur.

The shoulder joint is supported by ligaments, tendons and muscles. If these tissues are underused, overused or injured during a sporting activity, it is likely to affect your range of movement. The position of the shoulder may seem different to normal. There are many types of shoulder injury, the common ones are rotator cuff injury, impingement syndrome, frozen shoulder syndrome and winged scapular.

Rotator cuff injury

There are two different types of rotator cuff injuries. One is an acute sudden tear and the other is a chronic tear that happens over a longer period of time. The sudden tear might be from throwing a baseball or a fast punch. The chronic tear will begin as a dull pain that gradually worsens. The pain may start in the shoulder and gradually go down the arm, perhaps preventing you from moving your arm out to the side or above your head.

Impingement syndrome

This type of shoulder injury is commonly known as swimmer's shoulder or thrower's shoulder because it is often triggered off by the overuse of the shoulder in front crawl swimming or overhead throwing activities. The tendons of the rotator cuff become inflamed and don't have enough room for proper movement as they go through a narrow space called the subacromial space. Weak stabilization of the shoulder is the cause of impingement syndrome, and the best form of rehabilitation involves exercises for stabilizing the shoulder. Using a thera band is a good way to start rehabilitating a shoulder injured in this way. For both of these injuries, you should stretch your shoulder at least five times a day to help maintain the shoulder's full range of movement.

Common shoulder injuries

rotator cuff | inflammation of the tendons in impingement syndrome

thickening and inflammation of the capsule causing pain and lack of movement

raised shoulder owing to protrusion of shoulder blade

Impingement syndrome

Site of rotator cuff and impingement syndrome. The rotator cuff is vital for shoulder stability. Impingement syndrome is inflammation of the tendon, usually caused by overuse of the shoulder such as throwing a ball or swimming. Exercises using a thera band can help the injury.

Frozen shoulder

In the condition of frozen shoulder, the shoulder capsule thickens and eventually it is difficult to get any movement. Frozen shoulder can be extremely painful and movement in the shoulder is restricted. Regular stretching a few times a day can increase the range of movement.

Winged scapular

In the condition called winged scapular, the shoulder blade sticks out at the back causing the top of the shoulder to be elevated. The cause is usually an accident that damages a nerve that keeps the shoulder stable. Strength training and thera band exercises will help to remedy the problem.

Frozen shoulder syndrome

Despite years of medical research, there is, as yet, no specific explanation for the painful frozen shoulder syndrome. Internally, the lining of the shoulder capsule may thicken and cause scar tissue to form, which will then restrict the movement of the top of the arm bone. It is more common in men over 40, and in women generally. Poor posture and rounding of the shoulders may be a contributing factor. Eventually the pain in the shoulder will restrict sideways movement of the arm and any movements above the head, hence the term 'frozen shoulder'.

Rehabilitation will involve thawing out the shoulder in order to regain a full range of movement, which could take more than 12 months. Stretch the shoulder five times a day to maintain the range of movement in the shoulder.

Winged scapular

This is a visible injury – your shoulder blade will protrude at the back and cause the top of your shoulder to be elevated. This type of injury is most likely to be caused by sudden aggressive movements or accidents. The scapular becomes winged because the long thoracic nerve, which supplies the serratus anterior muscle, is damaged and can no longer hold the muscle in the correct position. This can be a painful condition, for example, there may be pressure on the scapular from the back of a chair. Also there can be limited elevation. In most cases, once the nerve has settled down, strength training is required, with back exercises to stabilize the scapular, such as single-arm cable rows, single-arm dumbbell rows, and bent-over rows. Use a thera band initially, working up to using cables and dumbbells.

Stretching and flexibility

Your shoulder muscles carry the weight of your arms all day and are therefore prone to fatigue and tightness. In addition to having to hold your arms up, the shoulder joint has to be able to rotate through 360 degrees, so flexibility in the muscles surrounding the shoulder joint is essential. Your shoulders should be pulled back for correct posture and to prevent problems with the rotator cuff inside the muscle. Also, pushing your shoulders back promotes even deeper breathing. Sitting all day with poor core-stability muscles and hands held forward on computer keyboards drags your shoulders up and forward, so do regular shoulder stretches throughout the day to prevent this.

Most gym users want to work their chest muscles, which normally involves some pressing exercises above the chest. This movement also contracts the muscles at the front of the shoulders and pulls them forward. Always stretch the shoulder muscles after these types of movements to counteract muscle shortening and keep it at optimum length.

Testing for flexibility

To test your shoulder flexibility, stand upright with your arms down by your sides, then slowly raise one arm, keeping it straight and your palm facing inward until it is beside your head. You should be able to take your hand through 180 degrees for good shoulder flexibility.

Cross-body stretch

This stretches the outside of the shoulder and arm. Repeat three to four times at regular intervals. If you feel pain, stop doing the excercise and try again at a later date.

Place the left arm straight across your chest and, with your right hand on the elbow, pull it across your body. Hold the position for 10 seconds. Repeat with your right arm.

Overhead shoulder stretch

Repeat this stretch three to five times to get a good stretch around the shoulders and upper back.

Hold your hands together with your arms straight above your head, pushing upward and backward. When your arms are at full stretch, hold the position for 10 seconds, then slowly bring your arms back down in front of you.

Swimmer's shoulder stretch

This stretch is a test of shoulder flexibility. Repeat three to five times for a good stretch. You can also do it against a wall.

Stretch your arm and place the palm of your hand flat against the floor. Press as close to the floor as possible – your armpit should almost be touching the floor. Hold for 10 seconds, then release.

Neck

Tight muscles in the back of your neck can cause your chin to push forward, while tight muscles in the front of the neck and top of the chest will drag your head forward and downward. Flexibility is important to help avoid overuse injuries and sports injuries.

Hands-up stretch

1 *Stand, with your feet hip-width apart, and your back flat against the wall, and position your arms up at 90 degrees, in a shoulder press position, with the back of your arms and hands flat on the wall.*

2 *Try to push your arms upward, keeping them against the wall all the time. Do not tense your neck. At maximum stretch, hold the position for 10 seconds, then slowly release.*

Thera band stretch

1 *Thera bands help you to follow a program using a suitable resistance level. Wrap the band around your hand.*

2 *Gently pull toward you and behind you. After a shoulder injury, use a thera band to strengthen the muscles.*

Sedentary lifestyles – such as those that involve staring at computer screens all day and overusing your neck muscles to hold your head in one position for long periods of time – will give you strong neck muscles but may put your head in the wrong position. The neck muscles then become stronger than they should be. While lifting heavy objects, the brain tells the body to recruit the neck muscles first before other muscles. If this happens, try to do more exercise and regular neck stretches to prevent the neck from tightening under muscular strain, and to keep it at optimum length.

Use these flexibility exercises to lengthen your neck muscles and position your head so that it is aligned with your pelvis to give you correct posture. At work, change your position regularly and ensure that you take time to do these neck flexibility exercises.

To check neck flexibility, stand upright, holding your arms down at your sides, with the shoulders back and down. Turn your head to look over your shoulder as far as possible before it starts to get uncomfortable.

Forward neck stretch

Keeping your back straight, slowly lower your chin toward your chest and hold the position for 10 seconds then slowly bring your head back up.

Sideways neck stretch

Take 4 to 5 seconds for each direction of the movement and repeat five to ten times. For a greater stretch, lean your head to one side, then raise the opposite shoulder up, then slowly down.

1 *Stand upright, head straight and your arms hanging down by your sides.*

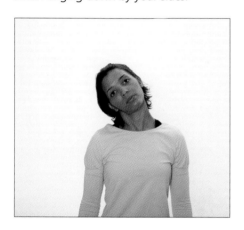

2 *Slowly lean your head over to one side and hold for 10 seconds before slowly bringing the head back up to the straight position.*

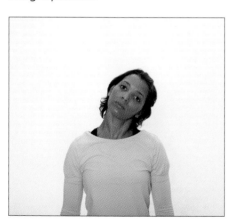

3 *Slowly lean your head over to the other side and hold for 10 seconds before slowly bringing the head back up to the straight position.*

Neck rotation

If possible, have your training partner massage your neck as you are doing this rotation. This should create a better stretch, as your muscles will feel much more relaxed.

1 *Stand upright, head straight and your arms hanging down by your sides.*

2 *Very slowly rotate your head so that you are looking over your left shoulder, hold for 5 seconds. Keep the movement smooth, without jerking the head.*

3 *Slowly rotate back through the start position to the other side, and hold again for 5 seconds. Repeat five to ten times to each side.*

Neck and shoulder stretch

With this exercise, you can get your training partner to hold your arms back to achieve a greater stretch. You could also adopt the PMF stretch principle for this stretch.

1 *Hold your arms straight by your side, with your training partner behind you.*

2 *Let your partner take your arms back behind you and hold them gently until you can feel the front of your shoulders being stretched.*

3 *After 10 seconds, your partner should let go of your arms, allowing them to return to the start position. Repeat five to ten times.*

Back

The muscles in your back are some of the strongest in your body but you still need to look after them. The following exercises will help you to keep them flexible, allow them to recover from regular exercise and avoid injury.

Cross-hand hanging reach

This is one of the most relaxing stretches you can do. Repeat three to five times.

1 *Keeping your arms straight, and your feet firmly on the floor, hip-width apart, grip the frame of a weight machine with your hands crossed over.*

2 *Push your hips out behind until you feel the stretch in your upper back muscles. Hold for 10 seconds before slowly bringing yourself back up to the bar.*

Reaching forward stretch

Repeat three to five times.

Grip your hands together, then stretch your arms straight out in front of you at chest height, rounding your upper back. Hold the position for 10 seconds.

Single-arm back stretch

This isolates the muscles of one arm and one side of the back. Repeat three to five times.

1 *Holding all your weight with one arm, and your feet hip-width apart, grip a weight machine.*

2 *Lean back. When you feel the stretch in your upper back, hold the position for 10 seconds, then slowly straighten up.*

Bent-forward stretch

Repeat three to five times.

Bend at the hip toward the floor until you feel the stretch in your lower back and hamstrings. Hold for 10 seconds. Repeat.

Hanging stretch

This stretch will not only stretch out your lower back but also your arms and abdominals. Repeat three to five times each side.

1 *Hang from a chin-up bar, gripping with both hands. Hold the position for about 10 seconds, then relax.*

2 *Gently rotate, twisting to the left, holding the stretch for 5 to 10 seconds. Relax for a few seconds then repeat.*

3 *Twist back to the right, holding the stretch for 5 to 10 seconds. Relax for a few seconds then repeat.*

Common back conditions

The back is prone to painful conditions as a result of overuse or muscular imbalances in other areas of muscle.

Lower-back muscle pain
This may be the result of overuse, such as rowing twice as far as normal or a massive increase in weight-bearing exercise. Sometimes, sudden movements can cause lower-back pain when the muscles in the lower back are not warmed up, for example, bending over to bathe a baby. The baby may not be heavy but the muscles that need to recruit in the lower back are not switched on.

Your back is very strong but, occasionally, if you make it work too hard, and don't have the necessary abdominal and core strength, your back will respond by going into spasm. These spasms may also be the result of poor posture or poor technique – if a spinal joint is injured, the muscle surrounding the joint goes into spasm as a natural response to stop the injured joint moving. When you experience lower-back pain,

consult a doctor for treatment to relieve the pain. Once the pain has started to subside, do stretches every 2 hours. When you are pain free, do abdominal exercises to prevent the injury recurring.

Scoliosis
This is a curving of the spine, which is often caused by overuse of one side of the body. Participation in sports such as rowing, racket sports and throwing sports are the main causes. For example, if you hit a ball all day with a tennis racket in your right hand, the muscles on that side of the body will become much stronger and more developed than the muscles on the other side of the body. This will make the spine form into an 'S' shape and will cause pain in the back muscles. Do regular stretches on both sides of the body to prevent the muscles getting tight and pulling the spine in one direction. To help prevent the injury in the first place, or prevent it from happening again, do the sporting activity using

the opposite side of the body to keep the muscle balance. For example, throw the baseball with your non-throwing arm, or row on the left side of the boat instead of the right.

curve in the spine

site of lower-back pain

Above: Overuse of one side of the body causes scoliosis, a curving of the spine. Muscles in spasm cause back pain.

Floor rocks

This is a great way to help the spine relax and release muscular tension in the vertebrae. Repeat three to five times.

Lie on the floor on your back, take hold of your knees with both arms and pull them into your chest. Gently rock forward and backward ten times, keeping your abdominals tense all the time.

Back roll-up

Straighten your legs and take them over the head to create a strong stretch. Repeat three to five times.

Lie on your back with your arms flat to the floor, palms down, and lift your legs up above your head until you feel the stretch in your lower back. Hold the position for 10 seconds, then gently lower your legs to the floor.

Common back injuries

If you suffer from a back injury, it can refer pain to other muscular areas, such as the back of the legs or the pelvis, affecting pelvic alignment.

Sciatica

Pain referred from the lower back into the legs is called 'sciatic'. Usually, the pain goes down the back of the thigh. If the lower back injury is across the whole back, the pain may be in both legs but in severe cases, it can go farther down the back of

Below: The illustration shows the areas around the pelvis and lower back that may be injured in piriformis syndrome.

the leg. The tingling, burning pain is caused by pressure on a nerve in the lower back. Keep stretching the back of the leg and the lower back to maintain as much movement as possible. Once the pain has gone, start a core workout routine to prevent a recurrence of the injury.

Sacroiliac joint inflammation

These joints are based at the bottom of both sides of the back. If you injure them you may feel an aching or sharp pain that can restrict your movement on one side, due to the pelvis having become twisted. The core muscles surrounding the pelvis may not be strong enough or may have

become too relaxed; this is often the case after childbirth. Often in endurance sports, especially running, the impact and tiredness in the muscles will cause the pelvis to slide forward, while the twisting effect can cause inflammation in the sacroiliac joint. Stretch the lower back and tops of the legs to keep the range of movement. The pelvis may twist back into place on its own, or you may need a specialist to fix the problem. Do lots of core strengthening work to prevent this problem recurring.

Piriformis syndrome

This is more commonly known as pain in the buttocks. The piriformis is a lump of muscle deep inside the buttocks, which the sciatic nerve runs alongside. If the muscle gets tight, it puts pressure on the sciatic nerve, which causes pain down the back of the leg. Overuse of the adductor muscles in the inside of the thigh causes the piriformis to overreact and tighten. Massage and lots of stretching are essential to prevent this syndrome. To regain full strength, do regular stretches for the buttocks, and strengthen the muscles of the buttocks and adductors.

sacroiliac joint

piriformis

location of sciatica

Sitting on heels stretch

Many athletes suffer from lower back pain, which could be prevented by regular stretching to prevent a build-up of tension in the muscles. Repeat three to five times.

Kneel on the floor, then gradually lower your weight backward until you are sitting on your heels and you can feel the stretch. Keep your arms straight and hold them as low as possible, as if they were being pulled to the ground through your armpits. Hold for 10 seconds, then release.

Lying one-leg, cross-over stretch

This is a great way to stretch the lower back and buttocks and assess the difference in flexibility between one side and the other. Repeat three to five times.

Bend one leg and pull the knee in to the chest using the opposite hand. As it gets pulled in, pull it across toward your opposite shoulder, allowing your lower back to twist slightly. Hold the position for 10 seconds before repeating.

Bend sideways stretch

This stretches the sacroiliac area and the obliques. Repeat three to five times.

Standing upright, with your arms hanging straight by your sides, lean over to one side as far as possible. Hold for 10 seconds.

Trunk rotation

This is ideal for sports such as golf and tennis. Repeat three to five times.

Stand and rotate round to your side as far as you can without moving your hips. Hold for 10 seconds.

Chest

Upper-body strength training, many sports, and simply sitting with poor posture, can all lead to a lack of flexibility in the chest. Regular stretching will help you to maintain good chest flexibility and avoid injury.

A tight chest will pull your arms closer together, giving the impression of a concave chest, and drag your shoulders forward. This has the effect of producing a poor posture.

Most arm movements take place in front of the body, so it is no surprise that the muscles in the chest get tight. Sports such as golf require you to hold your hands close together, causing your chest muscles to shorten. Golfers and all other sportsmen and sportswomen should regularly stretch their chest muscles and spend some time doing back exercises to counteract the effect of the chest muscles shortening. People who want to build muscle in the gym normally spend a lot of time doing chest exercises because the chest is a large muscular area in which it is easy to see improvements in size and definition.

If training the chest is a major part of your routine, then make sure you do flexibility exercises for your chest between sets of chest exercises.

To test your chest flexibility, stand with your back to a wall with 60cm/2ft between the back of your heels and the wall. Keep your feet where they are and lean back so that your shoulders and back are against the wall. Next, bend your arms at 90 degrees against the wall, with your elbows at shoulder height and palms facing outward. If the flexibility in your chest is good, you should be able to get your forearms, upper back and head to touch the wall all at the same time, without feeling any discomfort.

Make sure to do regular chest stretches to improve and maintain the flexibility in your chest muscles.

Bent arm assisted stretch

Use isometric stretching for better results. As you feel the stretch, contract your chest muscles to resist it for 4 to 6 seconds, then release. Repeat three to five times.

Get your training partner to hold your elbows and slowly push them together behind your back. Hold for 10 seconds.

Rupture of pectoralis

This injury is likely to be caused by heavy weight-training, using exercises such as bench press or flies. It often occurs following a sudden increase in the weights that are being used. Always make sure your weight-training technique is correct and arrange to have a training partner to help you in case of a sudden injury. Activities that involve throwing, such as javelin and discus, are also common causes, as they require very explosive power across the chest muscle.

The pain is usually felt at the insertion of the pectoralis major with the humerus (top of the arm), but there will be effects over your whole upper body. You will notice an immediate loss of power when you try to sweep your arm across your body, your chest and upper arm will be painful to move or touch and there may be swelling and bruising. Rest for 4 to 6 weeks then do lots of stretching exercises. Start rehabilitation using a thera band: pull it across your body, then resist the tension on the way back. When you can do these exercises without feeling pain, you can return to weight-training, starting with light weights.

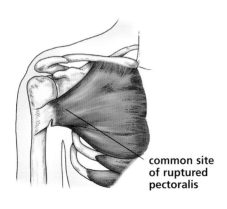

common site of ruptured pectoralis

Left: This illustration shows the area (shaded in red) affected by a rupture in the chest muscle (pectoralis). The rupture usually occurs at the junction of the pectoralis and the top of the arm. This injury causes loss of power, and rehabilitation can take several weeks.

Above: Once you are completely free of any pain after an injury, use a thera band with a suitable resistance to build the pectoralis muscle.

Fit ball chest stretch

To get an effective chest stretch, you can't just lean forward. You will need either some apparatus or a training partner. Repeat three to five times.

Get on all fours. Place one arm out to the side and rest it on the top of a fit ball. Lower your body until you feel the stretch in one side of your chest. Hold the position for 10 seconds before repeating.

Bend and hold chest stretch

If you don't have someone around or apparatus to help you, a stretch like this can be done in conjunction with a core exercise to make good use of your warm-up.

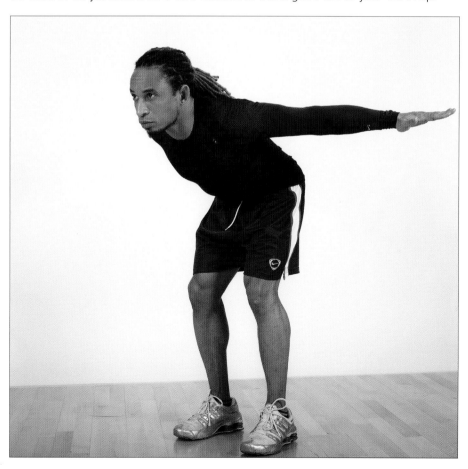

Bend at the hip and push your chest down toward the floor, keeping your arms straight out to the sides. Hold the position for 10 seconds before repeating.

Lying down assisted stretch

Use isometric stretching for a longer stretch. As you feel the stretch, contract your chest muscles to resist it for 4 to 6 seconds before release. Repeat three to five times.

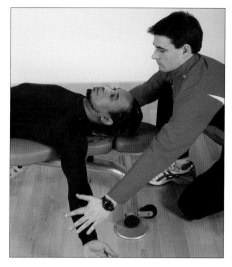

Get your training partner to stand behind you, to hold your forearms and push your arms toward the floor. Hold for 10 seconds before repeating.

Door frame chest stretch

This is one of the few exercises in which you can use your body weight to lean into a stretch. Keep your body straight from head to toe to promote a better stretch. Repeat three to five times.

Place your hands on either side of the door frame. Lean forward through the door frame until you feel the stretch in your chest. Hold the position for 10 seconds before repeating.

Upper Leg: Hamstring Stretches

The backs of the legs are used to control everyday movements and to provide power to go forward. The intense use of a large amount of muscle requires lots of stretching. If your hamstrings become tight, other parts of your body may also suffer.

Tight hamstrings can affect other parts of the body and cause problems with your pelvis and lower back. They will cause your pelvis to tilt and pull at your lower back, possibly leading to back pain and even sciatica.

Your pelvis needs to remain upright and aligned with the arches of your feet. Farther down the body, tight hamstrings can produce pain in the back of the knee and could also affect the calf muscles in the back of the lower leg, so that they tighten, thus preventing them from functioning normally.

Many people focus on exercising the fronts of their thighs in training because it's easy to see the muscles working and appreciate the developments in size and strength. This, however, can lead to poor balance between the muscles, hamstring tightness and possibly injury.

Keep your hamstrings strong with good training exercises and stretch them to maintain their optimum length.

Be careful not to overstretch your hamstrings – just get to the point where you feel the stretch. Making it painful will only activate the tendons at either end of the hamstrings muscle, which will prevent the stretch. Do not try to bounce in the stretch to make it go farther, as this could cause the hamstring to go into spasm and cause damage. To isolate the stretch to the hamstrings, tense your core muscles to prevent your lower back from moving.

To test your hamstring flexibility, lie on your back and push one leg into the floor. Keep it there while you raise the other leg, keeping it straight. For good hamstring flexibility, you should be able to get the leg you are raising to go past 90 degrees.

Standing hamstrings stretch

This will stretch the lower hamstrings toward the back of the knee.

1 *Stand on one leg and place the other leg on a bench, keeping it straight. Lean forward until you feel the stretch in the hamstrings. Hold for 10 seconds before repeating, stretching slightly more.*

Hamstring injury

This is a common injury for those who participate in any form of explosive sport; it can also occur following excessive running, cycling or other cardiovascular activities. However, you are unlikely to experience a hamstring injury in the gym because you are in a controlled environment and you do not exercise with as much speed. Hamstring strain means that one of the three hamstring muscles has been injured (semitendonosus, semimembranosus and biceps femoris), which will give you pain, and possibly swelling, at the back of the thigh. It is common for the front leg muscles (quadriceps) to create a more powerful contraction than the hamstrings at the back of the leg, which causes a muscular imbalance, leading to a hamstring injury. Stretch the injured hamstrings as soon as the pain has gone to make sure that the muscles do not shorten.

semitendonosus

biceps femoris

semimembranosus

Above: This illustration shows the group of three hamstrings in the back of the thigh area that can be affected by injury.

2 *For better effect, gently twist your upper body across the leg you are stretching, slowly pointing your foot toward you.*

Bent-forward hamstrings stretch

This is a simple stretch that can be done anywhere. Repeat three to five times.

Put your weight on to your back leg and bend it as you lean forward over your front leg. Pull the foot of your front leg up toward you until you feel the stretch in your hamstrings. Hold the position for 10 seconds before repeating.

Assisted hamstrings stretch

This is a good opportunity to try some isometric stretching. With an experienced trainer to help, you will achieve a full stretch. Repeat three to five times, both legs.

1 *Get your training partner to lift one leg up and push it back toward you until you feel the stretch. (Your partner should know when you feel the full stretch, because your other leg will automatically start to lift off the bench.) Hold the position for 10 seconds before repeating.*

Sitting hamstrings stretch

With stretches like this it is easy to overstretch. Just get to the point where you feel tightness. Repeat three to five times.

1 *Sit on the floor, pushing the back of your knees into the floor, and lean forward to touch your toes with both hands until you feel the stretch in the hamstrings. Hold the position for 10 seconds before repeating.*

2 *To make the stretch more effective, repeat the exercise as in step 1, but this time, as you reach to touch your toes, point your feet back toward you. This will stretch the lower hamstrings toward the back of your knees.*

2 *To bring the stretch lower down the back of your leg, assume the same position as in step 1 but get your partner to put pressure on your toes once you are in the stretch. As you feel the stretch, contract your hamstring muscles for 4 to 6 seconds, then relax before repeating.*

Thera band or towel stretch

You can do this stretch without a partner. Repeat three to five times, both legs.

Lie on your back on a mat on the floor, loop the thera band or towel around one foot and raise your leg straight into the air, keeping your other foot on the ground, until you feel the stretch in your hamstrings. Hold for 10 seconds before repeating. Then, repeat with the other foot.

Upper Leg: Stretches

The adductor muscles in the groin, the hip flexors and the gluteus muscles are all susceptible to strains and tears if they are overused repetitively, or are subject to powerful movements. Staying flexible can help you to recover from injuries.

Any sport or serious training places significant stress on the muscular regions that control movement at the centre of your body. As the intensity and speed increases, so too does the stress on the muscles around the area.

Your gluteus muscles, hip flexors and inner thigh muscles have to provide power as well as maintaining the stability that your other limb muscles rely on. These stretches should take priority and become part of a regular daily routine.

If the gluteus muscles get tight, they could cause your hamstrings and lower back to tighten also. The gluteus muscles are so big that they are often difficult to stretch once they are already too tight. The way to prevent this happening is to stay flexible.

Your hip flexors are susceptible to becoming very tight if you live a sedentary life. They should not stay in a seated position for long, or they will naturally shorten. But as soon as you need these muscles for walking, running

or any sporting activity, they will be too short. Make sure you stretch these muscles after long periods of sitting down, especially if you want to be able to run without injury. If they stay tight, they will eventually pull your pelvis down and forward, causing your lower back to arch more than it should, which could lead to lower back pain.

Your inner thigh muscles control fast powerful movements in your legs. They will tighten after exercise and shorten. Keep them long with regular stretching.

Common upper leg injuries

The following injuries are likely to occur due to lack of strength and flexibility, or a change in speed or stride strength.

Adductor tears
These are more commonly known as groin strains. They usually occur during explosive aggressive movements, such as sprinting, hurdling and changing direction in ball sports. A tear or rupture to any of the adductor muscles (brevis, longus, magnus, pectineus and gracilis) will cause a sudden pain in the groin area and loss of strength and control of inner thigh movements. You can expect

Below: The location of the adductor muscle tears and the hip flexor strains are shown in red.

to see some swelling if it is a rupture. Often the top of the leg will need to be taped to the waist to restrict the outward movement of the leg. Have regular massage to restrict muscles in the surrounding area from tightening and causing more tension on the adductor muscles. Once the swelling has reduced and the pain has gone, you can begin a regular stretching routine with a groin stretch before (when you are warmed up) and after any sporting activity. Add adductor and abductor exercises, such as fit ball inner thigh squeezes.

Hip flexor strains
Overuse of the hip flexors, caused by excessive cycling or running (especially if you are doing hill intervals or speed sessions) will make you prone to this type of injury. You will feel pain in the hip flexors and you may find walking difficult as you will have lost strength and the ability to bring your leg forward. You will also feel the pain as you stretch your leg back behind you. Start stretching the hip flexors as soon as the pain has gone but don't start running until you have strengthened them. Swimming and cycling are good ways to regain fitness, as these forms of exercise involve a shorter stride pattern and no impact.

Hurdle stretch

This also stretches the hip flexors of the bent leg. Repeat three times.

Sit on the floor, with one leg bent behind you, stretch forward, reaching toward your straight leg until you feel a stretch in the hamstrings of the straight leg and the groin area of the bent leg. Hold for 10 seconds then repeat on the other side.

area of hip flexor strains

adductor tears

Effective stretching
For any lower body stretches, do the movements in a slow and controlled manner. If a muscle is already tight the weight of the upper body forcing the stretch on the lower body can cause injury if done quickly. After holding the stretch the same muscles won't get you out of the stretch. Use your arms to relieve the stretch. Using the same muscles that have just been stretched will defeat the object of the stretch.

Inner thigh stretch

Training that demands speed and change of direction leaves the inner thigh muscles prone to tightness. Repeat three to five times.

From a standing position, bend one leg, taking your body weight over to one side until you feel the stretch in the inner thigh of the opposite leg. Hold the position for 10 seconds before repeating.

Groin stretch

The groin is always under a lot of pressure to help stabilize the pelvis. Repeat three to five times.

Slowly push the outside of your knees down toward the floor until you feel the stretch in the groin and inner thighs. Hold the position for 10 seconds before repeating.

Gluteus split-feet stretch on all fours

The muscles in the buttocks are in constant tension so they need good flexibility. Repeat three to five times.

Get on all fours with your knees close together. Force your feet apart and hold this position as you push your hips back toward your feet. When you feel the stretch in the hamstrings and buttocks, hold the position for 10 seconds before repeating.

Kneeling hip flexor stretch

Sedentary lifestyles cause the hip flexor to shorten, causing back and pelvis pain, and injury. Repeat three to five times.

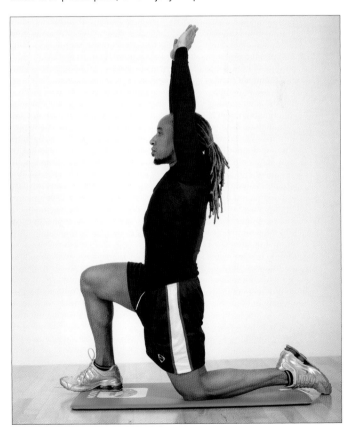

Kneeling on one knee, keep your body weight central and pull your pelvis forward until you feel the stretch in your hip flexor. Hold the position for 10 seconds before repeating.

Knee

The muscles attached to the knee in the front of the upper leg contract with a great deal of force and, therefore they tighten easily. To get the most out of these muscles, it is advisable to stretch them regularly using the range of exercises given here.

As there are many big muscles attached to the knee, it has to cope with a lot of stress, which can sometimes lead to injuries. Often knee injuries are caused by muscle imbalances elsewhere in your body. For example if your left buttock is weak, the muscles on the outside of the left leg will be tight. In time, they will pull at the knee to compensate for the weak buttocks. Use an expert sports physician to help you understand where the knee pain originates.

The force exerted by the muscles above and below the knee can cause injury to the tissues surrounding the knee through overuse or sudden aggressive movements. The knee joint relies on the muscles on both the inside and the outside of the thigh to keep the knee on the right track. The muscles located in the outside of the upper thigh are used in almost every leg movement. These muscles consist of a large mass that is unfortunately hard to stretch.

This part of the leg provides a lot of power and can often cause problems with the knee joint and even injury if it is not kept flexible. However, the muscle on the outside of the thigh is larger and more powerful than those on the inside of the knee, which can lead to the knee being dragged across to the outside, if the muscle on the outer area of the knee tightens through overuse. Consistent, repetitive exercise will inevitably make this happen, so make sure you do some of these stretches regularly to prevent injuries and poor performance.

Above: Cable leg extensions are a good exercise to strengthen the muscles above the knee.

Common knee injuries

The following injuries can occur as a result of repetitive movements, accidents and sudden, twisting movements.

Housemaid's knee
Also known as prepatella bursitis, it is often caused by direct impact to the knee or excessive kneeling. You may not experience pain at the front of the knee unless the bursa, a fluid-filled pouch at the front of the knee, enlarges and restricts movement. Stretch the quadriceps muscles to prevent them from tightening and pulling at the knee.

Dislocation of kneecap
This can be a recurring problem. It may happen at any time but most commonly occurs with sudden movement to change direction. You will instantly feel pain at the front of the knee and, in most cases, the kneecap will be out of its normal position. You may get further pain from other areas of the knee due to the change of position, and tendons and ligaments being stretched. Usually, the kneecap is pulled out of position by the quadriceps muscles, which contract due to weakness in the inside muscle of the quadriceps. The unequal force in the muscle will cause the kneecap to move sideways. Once the kneecap is back in place, keep stretching the quadriceps muscles, and get regular sports massages to balance the quadriceps muscles.

Cartilage pain
If the cartilage tissue – the knee's shock absorber – is torn, pain and swelling will occur immediately and it may feel as if your knee is locked. You will not be able to get much range of movement of the knee due to the swelling and the pain may continue to get worse. Once you have recovered, resume exercising with light stretches on the upper-leg muscles and exercises such as half squats and leg extensions using cables before moving on to free and machine weights.

Patella tendinitis
This injury is common in sports requiring repetitive movement, such as running and cycling. It is caused by overuse or overload of the tendon when bending the knee. You will feel pain just below or above the front of the knee and the pain will worsen as you squat. It is usually most painful in the morning, but improves as the day goes on.

Below: Several conditions can affect the knee, causing pain and discomfort.

patella tendinitis

housemaid's knee

kneecap dislocation

cartilage pain

Standing quadriceps stretch

For a more effective movement, push your hips forward once you are in the stretch. Repeat three to five times, both legs.

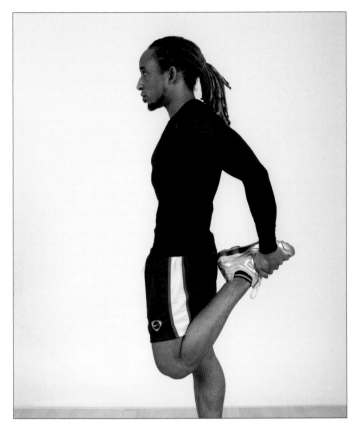

Stand up, bend forward and hold the calf of your left leg with your left hand. Pull the leg up behind you until you feel the stretch in the front of your thigh. Hold the position for 10 seconds before repeating.

Seated quadriceps stretch

This stretch helps to stretch out your abdominal muscles and hip flexors. Repeat three to five times.

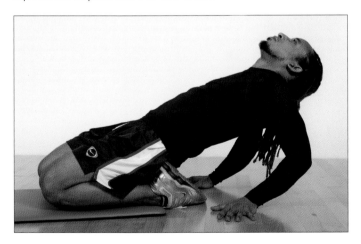

Kneeling on the floor, slowly lower your body weight back on to your heels, leaning your upper body backward as far as you can go. Once you feel the stretch in the front of your thighs, hold the position for 10 seconds before repeating.

Bench quadriceps stretch

If you suffer from back injuries, use this exercise to stretch your quadriceps. Repeat three to five times, both legs.

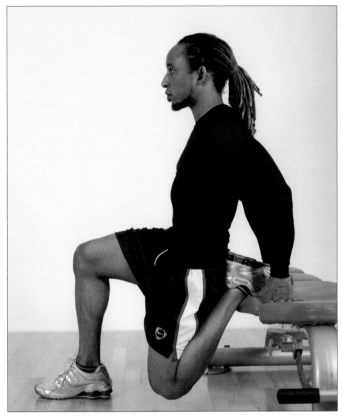

Hunker down in front of the bench, one foot flat on the floor and the other bent up behind you on the bench. Gently lean back to put more weight on the back leg and force the stretch in the quadriceps. Hold for 10 seconds before repeating.

Assisted quadriceps stretch

For a more effective stretch, use isometric stretching. Repeat three to five times, both legs.

Lie on the floor, face down, and get your training partner to bend one leg up behind you until you feel the stretch in the front of your thigh. Contract your quadriceps for 4 to 6 seconds to resist the stretch before releasing and repeating.

Sports knee injuries

Medial ligament strain

The medial ligament supports the inside of the knee. Contact sports and swimming, particularly breaststroke, where the knee twists each time you kick, can cause damage to this ligament. If the injury is caused by sudden twisting, the symptoms will be acute pain and a swollen knee – the body's way of preventing further movement of, and injury to, the knee. An overuse injury will cause little pain to begin with, but it will gradually increase the more you use the knee. The kneecap may also feel a bit loose or off its normal line.

To avoid medial ligament strain, stretch the hamstrings and quadriceps muscles to prevent them from shortening and pulling at the knee. If you have injured this ligament, start exercising the knee with leg extensions and short squat type exercises as soon as the pain subsides.

Lateral ligament strain

The knee being forced outward causes pain in the lateral ligament. This happens in contact sports when people land on top of one another and legs are bent in awkward directions. You will experience pain in the outside of the knee and movement will be impaired, depending on the severity of the injury. Continue to stretch the quadriceps and wear a knee support to prevent too much lateral movement. Once the pain has gone, strengthen the ligament with quadriceps and abductor strength-training exercises.

Iliotibial syndrome

The large band of muscle that runs down the outside of the leg to connect the gluteus to the outside of the knee is the iliotibial tract. It can be damaged by overuse or changes in technique. If it gets tight, it will cause pain either in the underside of the muscle or farther down toward the knee. It may only be a dull ache at first, but can worsen. You are more likely to feel the pain when doing the activity that caused it in the first place. It may prevent you from striding out when walking and will limit your normal movements, for example, when squatting. Rest the leg and get sports massage to release the tension in the iliotibial tract. Start stretching the area as soon as possible.

Popliteal muscle problems

One of the smallest, not very strong muscles behind the knee, the popliteal muscle is nevertheless important for an athlete. The functions of this muscle are threefold: it helps to begin to bend the knee by unlocking the knee from full extension; when the knee is straight or in full extension, the upper leg rotates laterally on the lower leg if the foot is flat on the floor; and finally, it medially rotates the lower leg under the upper leg. This happens during running, when the foot of that leg is up in the air, ready for the next step. If the popliteal muscle is tight or shortened, the foot will not plant on the ground properly.

Cause of injury and treatment

Injury to the popliteal muscle is mainly caused by overuse, severe sprain or strain to the knee. The muscle can also be overstressed by running in old, worn shoes so that there is too much rotation on the lower leg. Wearing outworn shoes stresses the popliteal muscle and your body generally. If the muscle is tight, the foot will come downward on to its inner side (excess pronation).

Treatment is gentle manual trigger point therapy and ultrasound. Because the popliteal cavity contains many nerves and blood vessels, to be effective, the manual pressure should be light. After treatment, the muscle can be strengthened by using low resistance rotational exercises of the foot and lower leg at high repetition.

site of popliteal muscle

Above: The popliteal fossa is the hollow at the back of the knee that houses the popliteal muscle.

medial ligament injury

lateral ligament strain

iliotibial tract

Above: The red shaded areas indicate the areas of likely injury on the inside of the knee.

Above: The ligament on the outside of the knee (in red) can be forced outward, causing pain.

Above: The illustration shows the muscle in the leg that is often responsible for pain around the knee.

Outer thigh stretch

The knee joint is held in position by the muscles on the inside and outside of the thigh. You can use these stretches to prevent your outer thigh muscles getting tight and causing injury, especially overuse injuries and muscle imbalances. Massage helps to keep muscles supple. Repeat three to five times, both legs.

Cross your left leg over the right and use your right arm to pull the left leg across while you twist your upper body around to face to the left. When you feel the stretch in your lower back and down the outside of your leg, hold the position for 10 seconds before repeating.

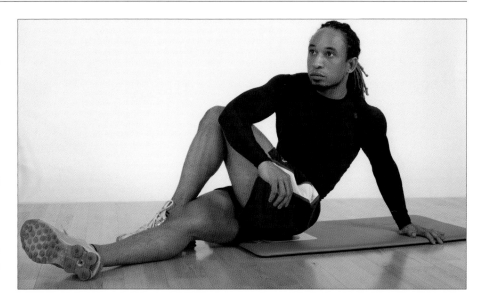

Standing outer thigh stretch

This stretch will help to relax the outer thigh muscles and also your obliques. Repeat three to five times, both legs.

Push your right hip out to the side, leaning your upper body over to your left side until you feel the stretch in the outer thigh of your right leg. Hold the position for 10 seconds before repeating.

Kneeling outer thigh stretch

The outside of the thighs are connected to the front of the hips by the hip flexors. This exercise stretches both areas.

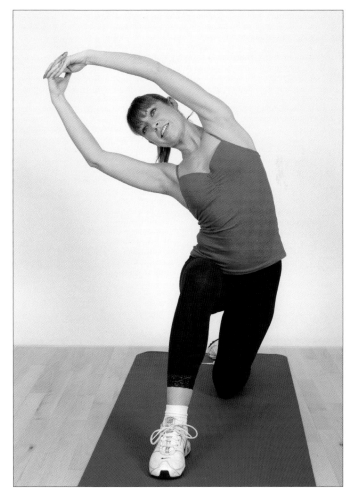

Kneeling on one knee, keep your body weight central between your legs and lean over to the other side. Once you feel the stretch down the outside of the thigh and ribs, hold the position for 10 seconds before repeating.

Ankle

Whatever training or sport you practise, you need to have good flexibility in the ankles, feet and surrounding muscles. Tight muscles will pull at the tendons in the ankles, causing a lack of flexibility and tightness in the soles of your feet.

There are more than 26 bones in your foot, and the sole of your foot has four layers of muscle and tendons. Treating feet with reflexology has taught us that tight feet and ankles can have an effect on the entire body. Regular stretching relieves muscle tension all over your body and will improve the function of your internal organs.

Farther up the leg, other muscles will have to work hard to compensate for poor flexibility in the ankles. For example, if your foot does not flex enough on impact while running, the muscles at the front and back of the lower leg will get overused, which will, in turn, cause injury. Because of poor blood flow to the

lower part of the leg, it can take longer to recover from injuries below the knee, so always make the time to maintain your ankle and foot flexibility. It is also important to ensure that the muscles in the rest of your body, especially the pelvis and lower back area, are relaxed in order to prevent them pulling at your foot and ankle.

Common foot, ankle and shin injuries

Foot, ankle and shin injuries are mainly caused by overuse or sudden changes in direction and balance. The following are some of the most common injuries.

Plantar fasciitis
This tendon runs from the heel to the front of the foot. It can become ruptured or inflamed, often due to overuse or a change in footwear with lower or higher arches than normal. The symptoms are pain in the heel that reaches the front of the foot. The arch of the foot tends to turn inward and collapse. To alleviate the symptoms, a doctor may tape the tendon to restrict its movement. You may need an arch support in your shoe to raise the arch of the foot and prevent it collapsing. Once you are free of pain, start stretching the bottom of the foot and the calf.

Below: This illustration shows the areas of the lower leg and foot that can be affected by injury.

Tenosynovitis
This occurs when the tendons on the top of the foot become painful as a result of inflammation of the sheath that surrounds the tendon. As well as pain, there may be swelling and there may be difficulty moving the inflamed joint. Tenosynovitis is caused by new footwear, wearing shoes that are too tight, laces rubbing on the tops of your feet, running fast downhill, running on uneven ground or excessive pointing of the toes. Don't do any activity or stretching until the pain has gone, then stretch with light toe raises and toe stretches.

Shin pain
The term given to a number of factors that cause pain in the shins is 'shin splints'. Symptoms of this condition may include swelling at the front of the shins, pain as you flex your foot and lumps on the front of the shin

bone. In most cases, pain is caused by inflammation of the periostium, a sheath that surrounds the bone.

To avoid shin splints, check your footwear to make sure that you have adequate support and cushioning for shock absorption, especially if you are running on hard or uneven surfaces.

Make sure also that your running technique is correct. Too much rotation of the hip can exacerbate the problem. If you do a lot of running, it may be worth seeing a professional who can assess your style and assist you with your running biomechanics.

Rest and ice the shin and the surrounding muscles to try to decrease the inflammation. Stretch your muscles at the front and back of the lower leg.

Ankle sprains
This common injury usually occurs when the ankle turns inward and the ligaments and soft tissues at the outside of the ankle are damaged. There are different levels of severity, depending on the amount of swelling and the range of movement you still have. Once the swelling is reduced and the pain has gone, start doing ankle stretches. Keep your ankle protected with a support at all times to restrict any sudden or big movements. Begin building strength in the ankle by balancing on one leg, then balance on a wobble board or BOSU (Both Sides Utilized) balance trainer.

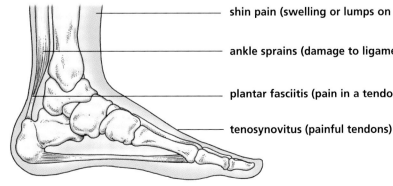

shin pain (swelling or lumps on shin)

ankle sprains (damage to ligaments)

plantar fasciitis (pain in a tendon)

tenosynovitus (painful tendons)

Ankle stretch

The tissues surrounding the ankle are likely to get tight during any exercise due to impact and change of direction. The ankles can suffer more tightness if you already have poor core stability. When the core muscles at the centre of the body are weak the ankles have to compensate farther down to keep stability. Repeat three to five times for each ankle.

Sitting on the mat, with your right leg out straight in front of you, grasp the middle of your left foot and twist it over to the right until the ankle is stretched. Hold the position for 10 seconds before repeating.

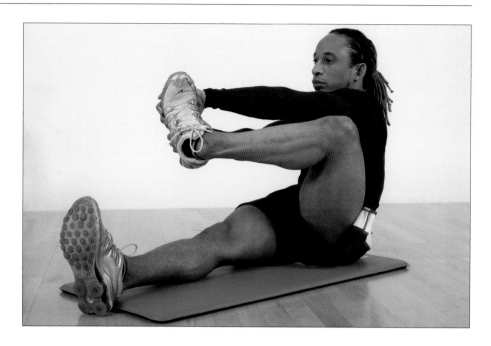

Ankle rotation

This stretch will move your ankle in all directions before exercise. Repeat three to five times for each ankle.

Standing upright, with your feet hip-width apart and arms by your sides, lift one foot off the floor and slowly rotate it in circles. Do ten circles in a clockwise direction and ten in an anticlockwise direction.

Foot stretch

Tightness around the ankle can cause injuries, so make time to do this stretch. Repeat three to five times for each foot.

Standing upright, lift one foot off the floor and point your toes until you feel the stretch in the front of the top of the foot. Be careful not to let your calf muscles cramp. Hold the position for 10 seconds before repeating.

Calf

Your calf muscles have to work hard throughout the day just to hold you upright when standing or doing exercise. The following exercises are suitable for maintaining flexibility in this crucial area and avoiding injury.

As calf muscles tire from long periods of standing and exercise, they start to tighten. When you are sitting, they shorten. If you do not spend time stretching them back to their optimum length, they will remain shortened. Tight calf muscles are one of the most common causes of Achilles' tendon problems. If the calf muscles are tight and you go to do exercise, the stress of the exercise will be put on the Achilles' tendon as a result of the calf muscles' poor elasticity.

Because of poor blood supply in the Achilles' tendon area, along with the constant use of your legs, it takes a long time for Achilles' tendons to recover from injury. Regular stretching to keep the calf muscles at their optimum length will prevent this happening in the first place. Tight calf muscles will also lead to tight hamstrings, making you prone to back injuries and tension in your feet.

As the calf muscle is made up of one part below the knee and another above, use a variety of stretches to maintain flexibility throughout the entire calf.

Common lower leg injuries

Strains are caused by pulling or twisting a tendon or a muscle. They occur as a result of overuse or training too much.

Achilles' strain and rupture
Ruptures are usually caused by a sudden acceleration forward while rising up on to your toes. This is a common injury among women who wear high heels and then play a game of tennis or squash or go running. The high heel shortens the calf and Achilles' tendon throughout the working day, then it has to lengthen for the sporting activity. Symptoms include a sudden sharp pain in the back of the lower leg followed by swelling; total lack of control of the back of the leg, and the calf muscles losing all strength and co-ordination; and being unable to walk even a few paces. A strain, or partial rupture, will result in the back of your leg being taped to restrict the movement of the Achilles'.

A complete tear will result in your leg being in plaster for six weeks or more. When the injury is starting to heal, do light calf stretches to get the range of movement back into the Achilles' and calf muscles. Wrap a thera band around your foot and pull it up toward you to get a stretch on the Achilles' and calf, then progress to standing calf stretches. As flexibility and strength improve, and you are able to walk, include some calf raises. You can put a heel lift in your shoe to relieve the pressure on the tendon.

Calf strains
Runners commonly experience calf strains, usually through overuse or a sudden increase in training load. Symptoms include pain in the calf muscles, which may go away when the muscles are warmed up, or get worse, depending on whether or not the muscle goes into spasm. If it does go into spasm, the blood supply to the muscles is restricted and the nutrients can't get to the muscles, causing them to tighten up. Have regular sports massages to loosen the calf muscles. Start stretching exercises soon after the injury to lengthen the calf muscle and prevent further tightening. To avoid calf strains, include calf exercises, such as calf raises, in your training plan.

calf strain (muscle may go into spasm to protect itself)

Achilles' strain and rupture (sharp pain and swelling in the lower leg)

Left: The areas that are white comprise the calf muscles and Achilles' tendon, which are both liable to injury.

Standing calf stretch

It is possible to stretch your calf muscles while you are in a standing position. Repeat the stretch three to five times for each calf.

Standing upright, slowly bend your back leg and push the back knee forward until you feel the stretch at the bottom of the calf muscles. Hold for 10 seconds before repeating.

Assisted calf stretch

Although you can stretch your calf muscles using your body weight and by creating an angle to get a stretch, it can be more effective to have a partner stretch your calf. In cases of injury and possible rupture to the calf muscles or the Achilles' tendon, assisted stretches when lying on the floor, are recommended. Repeat three to five times, each calf.

Lie on an exercise mat on your back and get your training partner to stretch your calf by holding your heel and pushing your toes up toward you. When you can feel the stretch in the calf, hold the position for about 10 seconds before repeating.

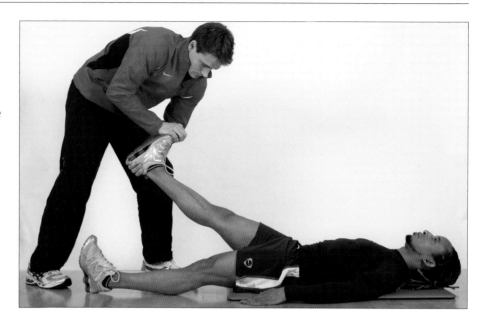

Step calf stretch

This stretch can be made more effective by doing it on one leg. Repeat three to five times for each calf.

Standing on a bench, with your heels just over the edge, and your arms hanging straight by your side, lower the heel of one foot down toward the floor until you feel the stretch in the calf. Hold the position for 10 seconds and repeat three to five times.

Calf stretch against a wall

For a more effective stretch, use isometric stretching. Repeat three to five times for each calf.

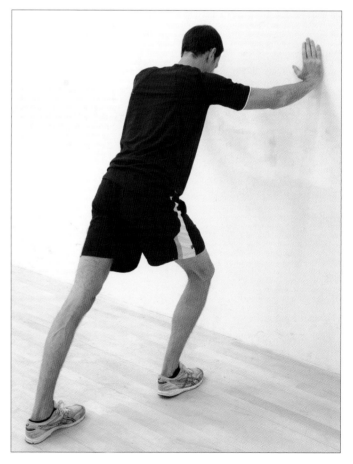

Lean face forward, palms flat against a wall, left leg back with heel on floor, and right leg forward. Slowly push against the wall to force the stretch on the calf. Once you feel the stretch, contract the calf muscles to resist it for 4 to 6 seconds. Hold the position for 10 seconds before repeating.

Arm

Upper-arm weight-training – particularly of the biceps – is a popular training exercise. To keep good flexibility in your upper arm, use the following stretches as a regular part of your training routine.

You use your arms in virtually every sporting activity and in everyday life. Most of us use our arms for small fine motor movements such as typing or texts and these smaller muscles in the arm can get overused. We are not designed to do constant small movements and the bigger muscles in the arms may suffer loss of tone and strength. On the sports field we expect our arms to provide strength to hit a ball, throw an object, punch or take our body weight. This can lead to muscle imbalances and susceptibility to injury. It is important to keep a balance. For example training biceps (at the front of the arms) will make the arms appear larger but this may create problems with the triceps (at the back of the arms). Weak arms may force other areas of the body to work too hard to keep up with the demands of the activity. An example would be using the neck muscles to lift a weight, rather than using the arms.

Common arm injuries

The upper arms are used in just about every training exercise, especially upper-body resistance training. They are susceptible to many different injuries. The following are just a few examples of the most common types.

Biceps and triceps strain
The usual causes of injury to the front and back of the upper arm are overstretching, an increase in workload and overuse. You will feel anything from a dull ache to a sharp pain, depending on the severity of the injury. Start stretching the affected muscle as soon as possible. When the pain has gone, begin strengthening exercises with light weights. Avoid sudden, loaded movements, such as hitting a tennis ball or throwing a javelin, until the muscle is strong again.

Tennis elbow – outside of elbow
Often the cause of tennis elbow is weakness in the biceps and forearms, poor technique or playing with a wet, heavy ball. The pain can be anywhere in the elbow, depending on which shot causes the pain. If you get pain when you play a forehand, it is medial tennis elbow, whereas pain on the backhand stroke is lateral tennis elbow. Avoid playing as aggressively as you did before until you are pain-free. Ask a tennis coach to check your technique – you are more likely to get tennis elbow if you play with your forearms and wrists as

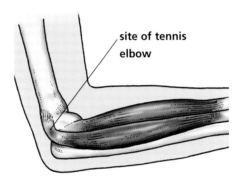

Above: The part of the elbow coloured red represents the area of intense pain when suffering from tennis elbow.

opposed to putting your shoulder and body into the shot. Use simple forearm exercises to strengthen the forearms and elbow: tuck your elbow into your side, with your elbow bent at 90 degrees and your forearm out in front of you. Hold a light weight and rotate it, starting with your palms facing upward, and rotating until your palms are facing the floor. Then, using the same arm position, start with the palm facing inward and pull your thumb up toward your forearm. Do three sets of ten repetitions for each arm, gradually increasing the number of repetitions.

Golfer's elbow – inside of elbow
This is similar to tennis elbow, although the pain is most likely to be felt in the inside of the elbow of the leading arm. It can be the symptom of bad technique and poor strength in certain areas, such as the wrist and forearms. This type of injury is also common in other sports such as baseball, in which the leading arm takes a lot of the impact when the club contacts the ball. Use forearm exercises such as this to strengthen your arm: tuck your elbow in next to your ribs. With your elbow bent at 90 degrees and your forearm out in front of you, hold a dumbbell or golf club in your hand and rotate the wrist with the palms facing upward to the palms facing downward. With the palms facing inward and the club held vertically, pull the top of your hand or thumb back toward you. Do three sets of ten repetitions for each arm, followed by stretching exercises to regain your full range of movement.

Forearm tenosynovitis
This injury involves the sheath of the tendon, where the forearm connects to the wrist, becoming inflamed and restricting the movement of the tendon within it. It can be caused by overuse of the forearm muscles, for example when gripping a racket or club too tightly. You will feel the pain whenever the tendon is stretched. Once the pain has subsided, do regular stretches on the forearms and biceps. To prevent forearm tenosynovitis happening again, make sure that the equipment you are using is right for you, and strengthen your forearms with biceps, triceps and wrist exercises.

Manual bicep stretch

To avoid your bicep muscles shortening, stretch between each set of exercises. Repeat three to five times, both arms.

Standing upright, hold one arm straight out in front of you, palm outward. Use the other hand to grasp your fingers and pull them toward the floor. When you feel the stretch in the biceps, hold the position for 10 seconds before repeating.

Assisted bicep stretch

For a more effective stretch, use isometric stretching. Repeat the stretch three to five times.

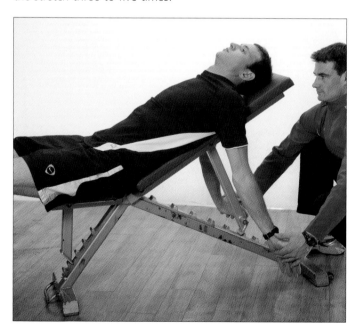

Sit on the bench, at a 60-degree angle, and get your training partner to grip your hands from behind, bending them backward until you feel the stretch in your biceps. Hold the position for 4 to 6 seconds before repeating.

Bicep wall stretch

When your arms are tired from training, use a wall to assist with a bicep stretch. Repeat three to five times.

Standing upright, facing a wall, place the palm of your hand, fingers pointing down, against the wall. Then pull your hand upward until you feel the stretch. Hold the position for 10 seconds before repeating.

Triceps overhead stretch

When training the chest and arms, stretch between exercises to keep flexible. Repeat three to five times for both arms.

Take one arm over your head and bend it at the elbow to reach the back of your neck and upper back. Push down on the elbow with your other hand, forcing the hand farther down your back. Hold for 10 seconds before repeating.

Abdominals

Your abdominals are in constant use, not just during intensive exercise, but also for everyday tasks such as going to the toilet or even just breathing. To get the most out of them, keep them flexible with these stretches.

When taking a deep breath in, you can help your chest space to open wider by tensing your abdominal muscles and pulling them in. As you breathe out, you contract your abdominal muscles to release all the air and make room for a bigger intake of air. For this to happen, you need your abdominal muscles to remain at optimum length so that they are fully functional.

Your abdominals are hardworking; they are subject to constant tension, to help you move in any direction, and to enable your pelvis to tilt and rotate in any direction. Your abdominals act as a corset to hold your body together and provide a strong solid base that other limbs can rely on. Without good strength and flexibility in your abdominals, your spine and pelvis would be unsupported, making you much more prone to injury. Your abdominals never rest – they assist your every movement and even work when you are sitting or lying down. Therefore, the abdominal muscles should be stretched regularly to help them maintain their optimum length and to function as best they can.

There are a number of flexibility tests you can do to see if your abdominal muscles are at their proper length. As many of these involve leaning backward, which can be bad for your spine, simply use torso rotation. Sit on a chair with your back upright and your feet placed flat on the floor in front of you. Cross your arms, with your hands on opposite shoulders, and then rotate your upper body as far as possible before you start to feel uncomfortable. You should be able to rotate through 40 degrees for good flexibility.

Stretch your abdominal muscles regularly, especially after doing abdominal exercises that tighten the muscles even further. And always stretch before sporting activities that require lots of rotation, such as tennis or golf.

Common abdominal injuries

When a muscle is stretched beyond its limits, the tissue can tear; causing a strain. This type of injury is often sustained during stomach exercises.

A hernia can result when the muscles of the stomach wall are weakened and allow part of the intestines to bulge through, causing a lump under the skin.

Abdominal strain

This is the inflammation or rupture of the stomach muscles that usually affects the rectus abdominis muscles in the stomach. Throwing events and other activities that involve aggressive, big muscular movements are likely to cause this type of injury, which can occur gradually or suddenly. Repeated abdominal exercises such as crunches and serving balls for tennis can

Below: The site of abdominal strain or rupture after heavy activity is the red area shown here.

rectus abdominis muscle (often the site of inflammation or rupture)

overstrain the muscles and cause a gradual pain after the activity. If you get a sudden pain in your abdominals, it is likely to be a rupture of the muscle. This is more likely to happen during the actual activity. The amount of pain will depend on the severity of the damage to the muscle fibres. In severe cases, the tear could cause some internal bleeding. You should immediately bend forward after the injury to prevent your stomach muscles from being overstretched.

After two days, if your doctor advises it, stretch the muscle by doing abdominal stretches to prevent the muscle fibres from shortening and causing further problems. Once the pain has gone, start to add more abdominal strengthening exercises to your routine. Always warm up before sporting activities and cool down afterward.

Hernia

A sudden increase in abdominal pressure can cause part of an organ or other internal tissues to come through a weakened area of the abdominal wall, causing a hernia. While hernias are not usually initially caused by sporting activity (although lifting very heavy weights can cause hernias), exercises that force big contractions in the abdominal muscles may make an existing hernia worse. Coughing and undue straining can also cause hernias.

Avoid doing any exercise until you have consulted your doctor, and only resume light exercise or training once the gap of the hernia has been reduced. Build up your abdominal exercises slowly, doing half the repetitions you did before injury until you get back to full strength. Do abdominal stretches every day to make sure that the abdominals stay relaxed, and to prevent any massive increase in pressure.

Abdominal stretch

This stretch is also a great way to stretch your hip flexors and quadriceps. Repeat three to five times.

Kneel on both knees on the exercise mat and lean back so that your buttocks rest on your heels, with your hands behind you on the floor for support, taking your upper body as far back as possible. Once you feel the stretch in the abdominals and hip flexors, hold the position for 10 seconds before repeating.

Above: Whenever you are lifting a heavy weight, the abdominal muscles will come into play in an attempt to protect your spine from injury.

Side stretch

Your abdominal muscles don't just work back and forth to do sit up movements, they control sideways movement as well. Repeat three to five times on both sides.

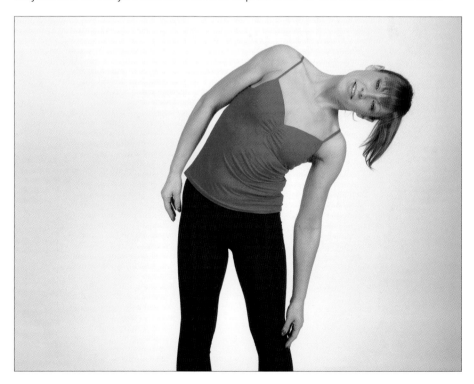

Above: As you stretch sideways using a dumbbell, your abdominal muscles will lengthen. On the way up, the muscles contract, to make them work harder.

Stand upright with your feet shoulder-width apart and lean over to one side to stretch the obliques. Hold the position for 10 seconds before repeating.

Common Muscle Injuries

Despite taking care when exercising and during sporting activities, backed up by regular stretching, muscle injuries do happen, and they can be painful and very debilitating. Here we look at some of the most common types of muscle injuries and their causes.

Repeated powerful muscle contractions can cause muscle cell damage, allowing calcium to flood into the cells, leading to cell death that peaks 48 hours after exercise. The body's inflammatory response stimulates the nerve endings in the damaged tissue, causing soreness that can last for a few days. This is known as Delayed Onset Muscle Soreness (DOMS).

A significant increase in training volume, participating in a new activity or heavy weight-training can all cause muscle soreness. Keeping your muscles hydrated will help the pain to subside; the discomfort is unlikely to last more than eight days.

Injuries

When working the muscles hard during training, there is always a risk of damage to muscles, such as pulling muscles or tearing them.

Acute muscle tears These tears can happen suddenly, causing severe pain, immediate loss of function and swelling. They can be caused by imbalances between opposing muscles (such as quadriceps and hamstrings), inflexibility, inadequate warm-up and muscle fatigue. The best treatment for acute muscle tears is the RICES method: rest, ice, compress, elevate and stabilize. Make sure that the tear has fully healed before attempting strenuous exercise.

Above: Muscle tears can be partial or complete. Whichever type they are, a total break from exercise is necessary to allow them to heal.

Chronic muscle tears These types of injuries are common among endurance athletes. The first warning sign is pain that builds up gradually after exercise. It may be possible to start another training session the next day but the pain will continue to get worse until it is impossible to train. The muscle may spasm to protect it from further use, causing more pain. You can tell what type of tear it is by pushing into the area with two fingers – if it is a chronic tear, this will be very painful. Stretching and strengthening your muscles before and after exercise will help to prevent this type of injury.

If you do suffer a torn muscle, apply an ice pack immediately to try to reduce swelling, and if possible, elevate the injured area. To prevent muscle tears during exercise, always warm up beforehand and every day.

Left: Using weights which are much too heavy for you will be likely to cause muscle injuries.

Above: Muscle cramps will play havoc with your training, so ensure you eat sensibly to combat the problem.

Above: Having a good warm-up before you start exercising can loosen your muscles and help you to avoid cramp.

Above: Understanding why you get stitches can help to prevent getting them again.

Cramps

There are a number of reasons for muscle cramps, which are involuntary contractions of the muscle. Dehydration, lack of essential minerals and low carbohydrate levels are among the most common causes of cramps, especially when someone is exercising or training hard.

Dehydration is a common cause of cramps, especially in hot climates. Try drinking 350–450ml/12–15fl oz of water every hour to avoid it. In very hot conditions, you will need at least 450ml/15fl oz of water per hour. Muscles work harder in hot conditions because your heart rate increases by roughly five beats for every 1 degree rise (1°C/1.8°F) in core body temperature, therefore muscles will be working that much closer to their maximum workload and will dehydrate faster, making them prone to cramp.

Essential minerals such as potassium and sodium are needed by the muscles to function properly. Low levels will result in cramp. Sports drinks that have a high potassium and sodium content replace the minerals lost through sweat, especially in hot, humid conditions.

Low carbohydrate levels can cause your muscles to fatigue faster. This in turn, can lead to cramp. Make sure that your nutrition before, during and after training is adequate to cope with the demands that you are putting on your body. Leave enough time after eating before you exercise to allow blood to return from the gut – where it is helping to digest the food – to the muscles. You may have to experiment with this – some people can exercise just 30 minutes after eating, while others need to wait a few hours. Try not to eat a really heavy meal if you know you are going to be training soon afterward.

Stretching

A warm-up that includes a variety of stretches should play a significant role in your weekly training plan. While stretching does not prevent injury, if you have limited mobility, you are more likely to get injured. If your muscles are already tight before you start to exercise, then they are more likely to cramp. There is no substitute for hard work – the more training you do, the better your muscles will be able to cope.

Stitches

There are two common types of pain that you may experience in the torso, commonly known as a stitch. If you eat shortly before exercising, your body will have to transfer blood to the working muscles rather than to the digestive organs, leaving the stomach full of undigested food. By waiting at least 90 minutes after a meal before exercising, you will reduce the chance of getting a stitch. If you are intending to eat during long-distance training, use energy drinks and bars that have been specifically made to aid digestion and release energy fast.

If, however, the pain in your stomach is not caused by food, it is probably a side stitch. This type of stitch occurs when you are exercising at a high intensity. The diaphragm muscles contract to a shortened position and are not able to lengthen fully. If you exhale completely, the diaphragm muscles will be able to lengthen and the stitch will start to reduce in intensity. To recover completely, you must breathe out forcefully and try to empty your lungs completely before you take in your next breath.

Fatigue and Illness

Sometimes, you may not be able to train. For elite athletes, rest is as important as training and plays an important role in avoiding injury. Here are some essential pointers that you can use to decide whether or not you really are fit enough to train.

When it comes to training and, specifically, avoiding overtraining, the simple rule to follow is: listen to your body. It is hard to tell yourself to rest when you want to get stuck into the next training session. The symptoms of overtraining that you should watch out for are: a dip in enthusiasm to train; heavy legs; breathlessness during low-intensity exercise; progressive weight loss; reduced appetite; and a resting heart rate that is five to ten beats higher than normal first thing in the morning and during steady exercise. Increased fluid intake and cravings for sugary foods can be another sign, as well as reduced sleep and bad moods. If you experience any or all of these symptoms, seek advice from your doctor.

Set your goals

To avoid overtraining syndrome, use a coach to help you set realistic short- and long-term goals. Keep in contact with your coach and keep a training diary so that you can monitor your training and recognize signs of overtraining. When your enthusiasm is running high, it is often hard to stop and assess how you feel and what you have done to make your body feel tired. It is likely that you will carry on regardless, taking no notice of the signs of fatigue. You may just assume that you are feeling tired because you are not fit enough, and then struggle on without realizing what's actually happening. This is a massive mistake. Your coach should be able to analyse your performance using measurements such as heart rate and tell you when you need to take a break.

Below: However fit you may feel, you are not invincible and should not train all day. Be realistic and take rests.

Above: Listen to your body and do not overtrain; it can cause unpleasant symptoms and even illness.

Above: If you are too ill to get out of bed, training will only make you feel much worse.

Above: Take the right medication to recover from illness faster, and take adequate rest, too.

A good coach, taking an overview of the entire picture, will be able to stop you overtraining before it really gets a grip.

Training when unwell
If you are suffering from a cold, and have a runny nose and a small cough, the chances are that your immune system is not badly damaged. You can continue light training, so long as you stop before you reach maximum intensity or failure. If you are weight-training, reduce the weights you usually use by 25 per cent to avoid any further breakdown of your immune system. If you are doing cardiovascular training, you may experience a drop in heart rate during interval training. Your body will not want to reach its normal level of intensity and its natural defence mechanism will prevent your heart rate from going above 90 per cent of its normal maximum. Your body needs to be able to fight the infection rather than use its energy to repair and rebuild muscle after heavy weight-training.

If the symptoms have worked their way into other parts of your body, causing you to feel run-down and achy, with a sore throat and headache, stop exercise altogether until you feel better. To get better fast, eat healthy foods, maintain your weight and get plenty of sleep. When you do resume training, exercise at a lower intensity and give yourself more rest days in the first few weeks, as well as more rest time between exercises and sets in the gym. Don't expect to resume your normal pace for cardiovascular exercise for at least two weeks.

Going forward
Ask yourself why you are suffering from overtraining or illness. Use your training diary to look back at what you have been doing so that you can avoid making the same mistakes. You may have increased your training too much over a short space of time, or the stresses of work or family life may have been making you particularly tired. Keep a record of your sleeping pattern, noting the time that you go to sleep, how well you sleep, and for how long. You can then check this record for irregularities.

Consult your food diary to see if you really are getting the nutrition you need for your body to cope with the demands of your training. Don't be afraid to be critical of yourself or ask for advice from a training partner, coach or nutritionalist.

When resuming exercise, take time to think about how you feel each day and listen to your body. Only change one thing at a time. For example, altering your diet, at the same time as including more intervals in training, can be too much for your body in one go, and it won't help you to pinpoint what it was that made you so unwell initially.

Below: Learn from your mistakes in training and resolve to take time to work on your weaknesses.

CORE STABILITY

Core stability is the strength of the muscles that hold the spine and pelvis in place. Without core strength, you will be prone to injury and poor performance. And the fitter, faster and more powerful you get, the more core strength you need to cope with the demands placed on your body.

Above: Maintaining a firm position to catch a medicine ball requires good core strength.
Left: Kneeling on a fit ball while holding weights demonstrates balance and stability, owing to core strength.

Importance of Core Stability

The term 'core stability' is used to describe the muscles of the trunk that hold and control the position and movement of the lumbar spine and pelvis. Because these muscles are rarely used in everyday life, they require special attention.

Thousands of years ago people had to be physically active to survive; our ancestors were hunters and gatherers who were constantly on the move, lifting materials to build shelters, tracking down animals for food and felling trees for fires. Today, we miss out on these everyday activities. In the past, we would regularly have used all the muscles that control the position and dynamic movements of the lumbar spine

and pelvis. Now, many people live a sedentary lifestyle and have little or no core stability.

You need your core muscles to be strong and active all the time for everyday movements. For example, if you are about to lift something heavy from the floor, your core muscles will have to tense before the rest of your body exerts itself to pick the item up in order to keep a brace-like position to

> **Working together**
> It's not just a case of getting your core muscles to work; they need to work in conjunction with your other muscles and recruit in the correct order to help all your muscles to be effective in establishing core stability in your body.

The core stability muscles

The major muscles in the trunk that provide you with good core stability are:

rectus abdominis

Above: *This muscle helps you to sit up.*

transversus abdominis

Above: *This muscle pulls you in and helps you exhale.*

multifidus

Above: *Controls movement of the spine in any direction.*

quadratus lumborum

Above: *Controls lateral movement of spine.*

iliopsoas

Above: *Flexes the tops of the legs and hips.*

external oblique

Above: *Controls lateral and rotational movements.*

internal oblique

Above: *This muscle controls lateral movement of the trunk.*

erector spinae

Above: *This muscle supports you bending forward.*

hold your spine and pelvis in place to assist the lifting movement. If your core muscles are not tensed, your spine and pelvis will not have the strength to maintain their correct position, leaving you prone to injury. Common problems related to poor core stability include lower back pain, rounded shoulders and back, and poor posture. With the appropriate core stability exercises, you will be able to recruit the correct core muscles to support your body effectively; the pressure on your back will dramatically reduce and your posture will improve.

Core stability is also important for optimum performance in many sports. You may have strong legs and shoulders but if your core stability is poor, the middle of your body may twist under pressure in a rugby scrum or tackle, for

Below: Sitting at a desk all day may result in your core muscles becoming even weaker.

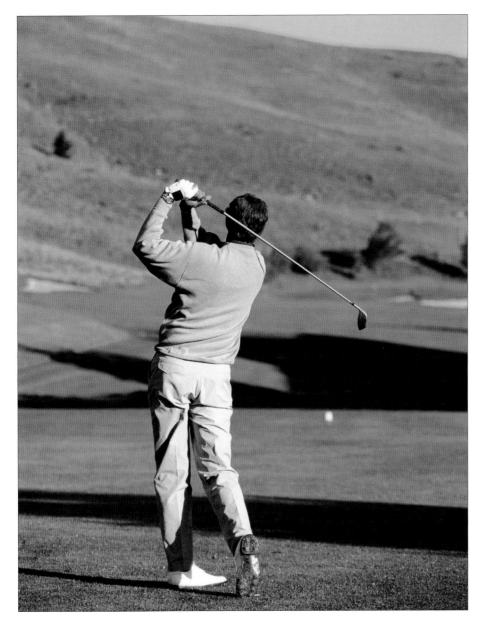

Above: An effective golf swing requires a good level of core stability to control the movement.

use in giving you good core stability, and, most people use poor technique when they do sit-ups and crunches.

Avoiding injury

If you are looking to build strength in your upper and lower body using weights, it is important to have strong core stability to avoid injury. Adding core exercises twice a week to your training programme will give you greater stability and power, and help you to avoid injury. Once your core muscles are switched on and recruiting properly you will feel them working. When you do a chest press tense the core muscles also. The muscles you are targeting in the legs or arms work harder and feel more isolated. Using the core muscles during other exercises will make them stronger and more effective.

Below: In combat sports such as rugby, strong core muscles are essential to avoid sustaining injuries.

example. Likewise, if your torso muscles are weak, your golf swing will suffer: you will not be able to transfer as much power from your body to the ball, and your lack of control in your back swing and follow-through will leave you off balance and at risk of injury.

People often make the mistake of thinking that simply doing lots of sit-ups and crunches will provide them with good core stability – and it's not true. It doesn't matter how many sit-ups and crunches you do, they will only help you to firm up your muscles to make it look like you have a toned, flat stomach. These exercises are, in fact, of very little

Measuring Core Stability

It is difficult to measure core stability and muscle recruitment outside a laboratory environment. However, there are some basic tests that will reveal whether your core stability is working efficiently enough to support you.

Core strength is so important that if the results of the tests below show that there is any weakness in your core stability, you should take time to work on all aspects of it. The tests not only reveal how much strength you have in your muscles, but also the recruitment pattern of the muscles connected to the core. If your core is weak, these muscles may not be recruiting effectively in the right order.

It is important to consider which core muscles are most important for your sport, and in some cases this means designing a test that is relevant to you. A good physiotherapist or expert in biomechanics should be able to tell you which parts of your body are the most important and which movements

---

Poor core strength

You may find you get cramp in your feet during these exercises – this is a sign of poor core strength, as your body has to compensate by using other muscles to keep your balance. If this happens to you, stop for a few minutes and try to relax your other muscles.

---

require help from your core-stability muscles. For example, in your golf swing, you need to have strong core muscles to prevent lateral movement at the hips. Doing a single-leg squat or lunge and watching the lateral movement at the hip closely will help you to see how strong your core is at maintaining the solid position required.

Film yourself from all angles doing the tests so that you can see for yourself where your core stability weaknesses are. Repeat these tests every six weeks to monitor your progress.

Below: You will be more prone to injury if you do not maintain core stability while you are training. A strong core is vital for effective exercising.

Ignore at your peril

Many people, including elite athletes, don't bother with core stability exercises, as it is difficult to measure the results. But core stability and correct muscular recruitment will relate directly to all sporting and exercise activities, so measure it, train it and monitor it.

Single-leg stand

Check your core stability with this simple test: Stand still for at least 30 seconds, without putting your arms out for balance. If you can't do this, your core muscles are not working well. In this exercise, all the core muscles are used.

Stand on one leg with your arms by your sides. Shut your eyes and stand still for as long as possible. As soon as you shut your eyes, you should feel your core muscles tightening – they help to hold you still, just like the guy ropes of a tent. Keep your feet as relaxed as possible to put more emphasis on the core stability muscles, thus making them work harder. Restrict movement in the hips when changing from one leg to the other.

Single-leg squat

Do this exercise in front of a mirror to assess which parts of your body are weak. All of the core-stability muscles are used in this exercise.

The lunge

In this exercise, the signs of a weak core are the same as those for the single-leg squat. Include lunges with leans and lunges with rotation in your exercise plan to make your core muscles strong enough to support your body in your chosen sporting activity. The lunge uses all the core-stability muscles.

1 *Stand up straight on both legs with your arms out in front of you. Balance well so the head is still (a sign of weak core stability is the head moving from side to side).*

1 *Stand up straight on both legs, with your feet hip-width apart and your arms hanging straight by your side. Try to keep the head and neck totally relaxed before you start the lunge.*

2 *Take a forward stride and lower your body weight by bending both legs, keeping your back as upright as possible. Try to avoid any lateral forward or backward movement during the lunge.*

2 *Squat until the thigh of your squatting leg is almost parallel to the ground. Pause for 2 seconds, then slowly stand up.*

Plank hand changes

Keep your core muscles switched on through this exercise. All of the core muscles are recruited for this exercise.

1 *Adopt the standard press-up position, with your legs wide apart and hands with palms flat on the floor, so that you can keep your hips still and progressively move your feet closer together to assess how much your core stability is improving. Focus on the hips and don't move them sideways or rotate them.*

2 *Slowly raise one hand off the floor and place it on top of your other hand. Feel and watch out for any lateral, upward and downward movement of the hips. Your core is working well when there is little trunk movement during the exercise. Lateral movement and/or rotation in the centre of the body will make you prone to injury.*

Check your core stability

Look out for the signs of weak core stability: head moving from side to side; hips dropping down and not staying level (also indicative of weak gluteus muscles); leg crossing behind your squatting leg during the squat (also indicative of weak buttock muscles); knee wobbling from side to side (indicative of weakness higher up in core muscles); and trunk constantly moving.

Basic Core Exercises

It is vital to begin with these basic core exercises in order for your core muscles to recruit correctly. If you jump to more advanced exercises, your core muscles will not benefit, and you will be prone to injury.

In addition to beginning with these exercises so that you can get your muscles recruiting correctly, you should also regularly revert back to using them to check whether you are doing the basics correctly.

If possible, you should also work with a training partner who can observe your exercising and give you some guidance on whether your core muscles are working properly. Where possible, try placing your hands on the core muscles you are supposed to be working during the exercise to see if they are held in tension or not.

For each exercise, take 2 to 3 seconds for each direction of the movement. Breathe out at the beginning of the movement, continue breathing through the hold, and breathe in as you return to the start position.

Think before you tense

It is easy to do core-stability exercises without knowing which muscles you are trying to engage. Take your time to think clearly about which parts of the body are giving you the stability for each exercise, and be patient, focusing intently on that part of the body. If you are in a position that requires you to hold the core muscles tight, then keep your body as still as possible.

Many people think they have mastered an exercise and quickly move on to more advanced core work when, in fact, they only keep their balance by wobbling from side to side, waving their arms around or holding on to a wall. If you are really struggling to feel your core muscles, especially your abdominal muscles, then try feeling them when you are coughing. The tension that you feel around your abdominal area as you are coughing is caused by the core muscles tensing.

Plank (prone bridging)

Muscles used Rectus abdominis; transversus abdominis; internal obliques

1 *Lie on your front with your legs out straight behind you and your hands clasped together in front of you, with your forearms flat on the floor. Keep your spine in neutral all the time and don't let your back arch.*

2 *Raise your hips so that only your forearms and toes are resting on the floor. Hold this position for as long as possible by tensing your core muscles. Push your chest out and keep your shoulders back to make the exercise harder. You should aim to hold the plank for as long as you possibly can. Begin by holding the position for 20 seconds, adding 5 seconds each time, until you can stay in this position for at least 1 minute.*

Plank to single-leg raise

Muscles used Rectus abdominis; transversus abdominis; internal obliques

1 *Lie on your front with your legs out straight behind you and your hands clasped together in front of you, with your forearms flat on the floor. Keep your spine in neutral and tense your core muscles.*

2 *Raise your hips, keeping your forearms and toes on the floor, then lift one leg off the ground, keeping it straight out behind you. Hold for up to 30 seconds. Repeat the exercise with the other leg.*

Side plank raises (lateral bridging)

Muscles used Obliques – internal and external; transversus abdominis

1 *Lie on your side, with the legs out straight, a forearm flat on the floor, with the hand in a loose fist position, the other hand palm down on the floor, and one foot resting on top of the other.*

2 *Raise your hips, keeping one forearm on the floor and your feet together. Raise the other arm straight up in the air. Hold so your body is in a straight line.*

Gluteal bridge

Muscles used Rectus abdominis; gluteus maximus; erector spinae

Lie on your back on a mat, with the legs bent at 90 degrees. Tense your core muscles, especially the gluteus muscles, and raise your hips until your body is level in one line, from your knees to your shoulders. Begin by holding the position for 10–20 seconds, gradually building up to a 1-minute hold.

Tips for core exercises
Start by keeping your body as still as possible, then begin tensing your core muscles. Try pushing through your heels to put more emphasis on the gluteus and less stress on your knees. Focus on tensing your buttocks. Keep your hands and elbows off the ground to make your core muscles work harder. Breathe out to begin and in when you return to the start.

Single-leg stand

Muscles used All the core muscles are used for this exercise.

Stand on one leg, with your eyes closed and both arms hanging by your sides. Try to keep your body still and as relaxed as possible, then tense your core muscles to maintain your balance. Hold your position for 10–20 seconds, gradually building up to a 1-minute hold. Keep your spine in neutral throughout the movement and focus on working the obliques. After you have completed a 1-minute hold, try holding the position for as long as possible, tensing your core muscles all the time.

Intermediate Core Exercises

As your core-stability muscles get stronger, you can start to introduce exercises –
of the kind given here – that involve making a strong connection between
your core muscles and the muscles of your limbs.

When you start using your limbs to press and pull weights, it is important to be able to keep your spine and pelvis in their natural positions in order to make your core-stability muscles stronger for everyday activities and sporting movements.

Remember that you are only as strong as your core-stability muscles. Without strengthening the core, you will not increase your physical power and will always be more prone to injury.

Taking your limbs away from the centre of your body will act as a lever to make your core muscles work even harder. Exercises that involve rotation will force some core muscles to keep your body still, with other core muscles working to allow parts of your body to rotate, but in a controlled way. If you don't take time to get this correct, other muscles – mainly in the lower back – will be forced to do the work, which will not give you the core strength that you are looking for.

For each exercise, take 2 to 3 seconds for each direction of the movement. Breathe out at the beginning of the movement, and breathe in as you return to the start position.

For the following intermediate core exercises, start with three sets of five repetitions and build up gradually over the weeks until you are doing five sets of ten repetitions.

Rest-day exercise

For you to get the maximum benefit from your core exercises, they need to be given your full attention and energy. At the intermediate stage you should try to plan two core-stability workouts a week. You need to do these sessions separately from your normal cardiovascular or strength-training sessions. Try fitting them in on the days that you would normally rest.

Plank leg kick

Muscles used Rectus abdominis; transversus abdominis; internal obliques; gluteus maximus; tensor fascia lata

1 *Lie on your front, legs out straight, hips raised, with forearms and toes on the floor.*

2 *Raise one foot, bend your knee and bring it in toward your chest until your thigh is perpendicular to the ground.*

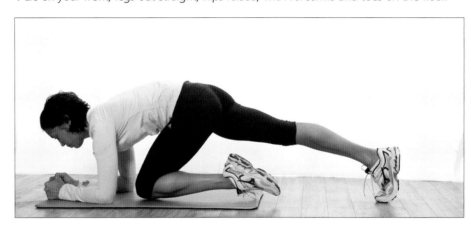

3 *Kick the leg back out, slowly but forcefully, until it is straight out behind you. Hold for 5 seconds, then bring the knee in. Repeat with the other leg.*

Hip-raise, single-leg changeovers

Muscles used Rectus abdominis; gluteus maximus; erector spinae

1 *Adopt the gluteal bridge position. Tense your core muscles, especially the gluteus muscles. Raise your hips until your body is in one line from your shoulders to the knees.*

2 *Slowly raise one leg until it is in line with the rest of your body. Hold this position for 5 seconds then change legs, keeping your hips off the floor and your body in line.*

Superman

Muscles used Erector spinae; gluteus maximus; rectus abdominis

1 *Start with your hands and knees on the floor, and your belly button pulled in toward your spine to keep your core muscles tense.*

2 *Raise your right leg off the floor, straighten it behind you, lift and straighten your left arm in front of you. Hold for 5 seconds, return to the start position and repeat with the opposite limbs.*

Cable wood chops, high to low

Muscles used Rectus abdominis; obliques – internal and external

Work the core muscles

Try to visualize a poker going through the top of your head and down the length of your spine. If you imagine turning on this 'axis', you will find that the exercise is more effective.

Use a weight that is lighter than you think you need to start with. Use a mirror to check your technique, to help you eliminate any lateral hip movement.

With rotational exercises, your hips will try to move. To create a strong core, keep the hips still; get the core muscles to work.

This is a great exercise for golfers as it involves the same muscles used for the golf swing.

1 *Stand side-on to the cable machine, with your feet just over hip-width apart. Turn toward the machine by twisting upward from just above the hips, and grip the rope in both hands.*

2 *Slowly rotate your upper body, keeping your arms straight out in front, until the handle is level with your opposite knee. Pause for a second, then slowly rotate back to the start position.*

Advanced Core Exercises

When you get to an advanced stage of your core-stability training, you can start to involve dynamic exercises that will simulate the movements you might use in your sport. These exercises make it hard to balance, so that your core muscles have to work hard.

Most people believe that you are either naturally blessed with having good balance or not, when in fact it really comes down to your core muscles giving you enough stability to achieve really good balance.

Most sporting movements call for good balance to cope with changes in direction and transferring weight and stress from one limb to another. Some of the following exercises use weights to make the exercise harder and to help build core muscles. If you want to move your limbs

with strong, rapid movements, you will need to have very strong core stability with great balance.

For each exercise, take 2 to 3 seconds for each direction of the movement. Breathe out at the beginning of the movement, continue breathing through the hold, and breathe in as you return to the start position.

For all of these exercises, begin with three sets of repetitions each side of the body, gradually building up to five sets of ten repetitions each side.

> **Exercise to stay injury-free**
> When you have reached the advanced stage, just build the exercises into your normal training programme. Do them between cardiovascular exercises and resistance exercises to help keep your core muscles switched on through all of your movements. It will also help you avoid injuries in training and make the core muscles focus and become recruited to support your limbs as they start to fatigue.

Two-point Superman

Muscles used Erector spinae; gluteus maximus; rectus abdominis

1 *Start on all fours on a mat, with both hands and knees on the floor, hands palm down. Try to prevent your lower back from arching.*

2 *Raise and straighten your right leg out behind you. At the same time, raise and straighten your left arm in front of you. Pull your belly button in toward your spine.*

3 *To make this a two-point Superman, lift the foot of your supporting leg off the floor to work your core muscles harder.*

4 *Hold for 5 seconds, then bring your right leg and left arm in until the knee and elbow touch. Repeat on the other side.*

Press-up plank to side waves

Muscles used Rectus abdominis; obliques – internal and external; pectoralis major

1 *Start in a standard press-up position.*

2 *Lower your body toward the floor by bending your elbows out to the sides.*

3 *With elbows bent at 90 degrees, hold for 2 seconds then push back up.*

4 *Take one arm out to the side and twist your body until you are side-on to the floor in a side plank position. Think of your trunk as a brace and don't let your hips drop in the rotation. Let your feet rotate over on to their sides.*

Single-leg cable wood chops, high to low

Muscles used Erector spinae; gluteus – maximus, medius; rectus abdominis

1 *Stand on one leg, with the other foot raised just slightly off the floor, side-on to the cable machine. Turn your upper torso slowly toward the machine and grip the rope with both hands. Try doing this exercise sitting on a fit ball, with only one foot on the floor.*

2 *Slowly rotate your upper body, keeping your arms straight out in front of you until the handle is level with your opposite knee. Pause for a second, then slowly rotate back to the start position. Keep your hips facing forward to put greater emphasis on the core muscles.*

Superman row

Muscles used Erector spinae; rectus abdominis; obliques; latissimus dorsi

1 *Stand on one leg and hold your other leg straight out behind you, and your opposite arm straight out in front of you. Hold a dumbbell in the other hand at knee height. Keep your back parallel to the floor.*

2 *Pull the dumbbell up to your ribs, taking your elbow past your ribs and back behind the line of your body. Avoid twisting your trunk as you pull the weight up. Pause for 1 second, then return to the start position.*

Fit Ball Core Exercises

The fit ball is an effective piece of equipment for improving core stability, because it forces your body to stimulate more neuromuscular pathways, which in turn activate a larger number of muscle fibres in the core.

The fit ball was first introduced in the 1980s as a way of improving posture and rehabilitation for injuries. But because the fit ball helped to achieve great results in increased core stability among top athletes, it has become a great tool for people of all abilities.

Being round, a fit ball is an unstable surface to work on, unlike a conventional flat bench in the gym. As a result, core-stability muscles have to stay switched on throughout any movement when you are on the fit ball if you want to stay on the ball. Just sitting on a ball holding your body upright requires the majority of your core-stability muscles to work. The ball also allows you to get a greater range of movement for exercises that you would usually do on the floor. For example, with gluteal bridges, you can lower your hips to the ground before tensing them to come back up.

By using a fit ball, your body awareness and balance will improve, which is a bonus for any sporting activity. Do not try using these exercises until you have completed the intermediate stage of your core-stability training.

Building connections

Replace some of your regular gym exercises with fit ball exercises to build the connection between your core and limbs. For example, when training your legs, include some single-leg fit ball squats; for a chest session, include fit ball press-ups; and for a shoulder workout, include some fit ball shoulder presses. Many of the exercises used in the gym can be replicated using the fit ball; this will make them significantly harder and ensure that you are using your core muscles correctly. Many world-class athletes have stated that using a fit ball made a big difference to their performance.

Fit ball hip raises, feet on ball

Muscles used Gluteus maximus and medius; rectus abdominis; obliques – internal and external; biceps femoris

1 *Lie on your back on a gym mat on the floor, with your feet on the top of the fit ball and your hands flat on the floor, palms down. Tense your core muscles, especially your buttocks. Keep the ball as still as possible.*

2 *Raise your hips until your body is in one line from your shoulders to your knees. Try to maintain your balance throughout. Hold this position for 5 seconds, then slowly return to the start position.*

Single-leg fit ball squat

Muscles used Rectus abdominis; gluteus medius; quadriceps

1 *With the fit ball between your lower back and a wall, slowly squat in front of a mirror, pushing your weight through your heels, until your heel is almost parallel to the floor.*

2 *Pause for 2 seconds, check that your hips are staying in line, then gradually extend your legs until you are standing fully upright. Tense your buttocks as your legs straighten.*

Fit ball plank

Muscles used Rectus abdominis; transversus abdominis; internal obliques

Adopt a plank position with your elbows and forearms resting on the ball and your feet out behind you, resting on your toes. Hold this position for as long as possible by tensing your core muscles. Keep your spine in neutral all the time and don't let your back arch. If your back does start to arch, stop the exercise immediately; it will have a negative effect by teaching your body to do the exercise using the wrong muscles. Aim to hold the plank for as long as possible. Begin by holding the position for 20 seconds, building up to a 1-minute hold for three sets.

Fit ball side roll

Muscles used Obliques; gluteus medius; rectus abdominis; tensor fascia lata

1 Rest the fit ball under your shoulders and neck. Keep your knees bent at 90 degrees and your feet flat on the floor. Tense your core muscles to keep your hips up in line with your knees and shoulders. Look down toward your feet to help you balance at first. Focus on working your obliques and gluteus medius.

2 Roll your upper body over to one side of the fit ball until you reach the point where you start to lose your balance. Pause for 2 seconds, then slowly return to the start position. Start with your feet wide apart and gradually bring them closer together as you get better at the exercise. Start with three sets of five repetitions to each side.

Fit ball shoulder press

Begin with three sets of five repetitions, then build up to five sets of ten repetitions.

Muscles used Rectus abdominis; gluteus – maximus and medius; deltoid

1 Holding dumbbells in each hand, sit on the fit ball, raise one foot off the floor and lift the dumbbells up to ear level. Have a training partner close to you throughout this exercise to help you get used to balancing on the ball.

2 Keeping your core tensed, raise the dumbbells up above your head, pause for 2 seconds, then slowly return to the start position.

BOSU Core Exercises

The BOSU, an acronym for Both Sides Utilized, is an excellent tool for recruiting and strengthening your core muscles. Every time you move on a BOSU you have no choice but to switch on your core muscles in order to maintain balance and co-ordination.

When using either side of the BOSU (one side has a flat base and the other is similar to a rounded jelly), the slightest movement will force your core muscles to work, thereby strengthening the connection between your limbs and core muscles. For each exercise, take 2 to 3 seconds for each direction of the movement. Breathe out at the beginning of the movement, throughout the hold, and in as you return to the start position.

BOSU plank knee tuck with rotations

Muscles used Rectus abdominis; transverse abdominis; gluteus – maximus and medius

1 *Adopt the standard plank position, firmly gripping the sides of the BOSU with your hands and keeping your core muscles tense, so that you can raise your body upward on to your toes. Keep the shoulders level so the core works harder.*

2 *Raise one leg until the knee touches the opposite elbow, your trunk rotating slightly to get the full range of movement. Pause for 2 seconds, then return to the start. Begin with three sets of five repetitions. Build up to three sets of 15 on each side.*

BOSU Superman

Muscles used Rectus abdominis; transverse abdominis; and gluteus – maximus and medius

1 *Position yourself carefully on all fours on the BOSU so that you can maintain your balance. Pull your belly button in to maintain a flat back and keep your head in line with your spine. Keep your core muscles tense all the time to keep your spine in neutral.*

2 *Raise your left leg and straighten it out behind you. At the same time, extend your right arm in front of you. Hold this position for 5 seconds, then return to the start position. Keep breathing during the exercise. Start with five repetitions, change limbs and build up to twenty repetitions on each side.*

BOSU squat

Muscles used Rectus abdominis; transverse abdominis; gluteus – maximus and medius; quadriceps

1 *Start by placing one foot on the BOSU, allowing it to rock to one side, then slowly add your other foot and attempt to find your balance. Get your training partner to help you to balance if it's the first time you have tried using the BOSU.*

2 *Squat down slowly until your thighs are parallel with the floor. Pause for 2 seconds, then slowly extend your legs and stand upright. When you can keep your balance and there is no visible wobble, try squatting on one leg to place greater emphasis on your gluteus medius. Begin with three sets of five repetitions, building up to three sets of twenty repetitions.*

Cable wood chop on BOSU, high to low

Muscles used Gluteus medius; obliques

1 *Begin with a light weight and practise keeping the top of the BOSU as flat as possible as you rotate, before progressing to heavy weights. Stand on both feet, facing forward on the BOSU, then twist your upper torso toward the cable machine. Grip the rope in both hands.*

2 *Slowly rotate using core muscles, taking the cable across your body until it is level with your opposite knee. Pause for 1 second, then slowly rotate back to the start position. This exercise is a great one for golfers, as the rocking motion of the BOSU is similar to the lateral movement needed when swinging a golf club.*

BOSU lat pull-down

Muscles used Latissimus dorsi; transverse abdominis

1 *Stand on the BOSU and grip the rope with both hands.*

2 *Pull the rope in toward the bottom of your chest, taking your elbows out to the side.*

Combination exercises

You can introduce these BOSU core exercises on their own or use them in conjunction with and to advance your normal resistance exercises. The BOSU can be used in conjunction with other core-stability exercises to make them harder. For example, doing fit ball press-ups with your feet resting on the flat side of the BOSU.

Medicine Ball Core Exercises

Medicine ball exercises are an effective and fun way to work your core muscles. The exercises given here will also help you to develop power, co-ordination and balance, all of which are important in most sporting activities.

If you are trying to catch or throw a medicine ball, you are forced to tense your core muscles in order to take the impact of the throw when catching it. You are also compelled to tense your core muscles to brace your body to hold it still while releasing it in the throw. Having a stable base for most sports is essential. If you use the ball in exercises that involve big movements, your core muscles will have to work against the inertia of the ball when moving it. Medicine ball exercises can also teach your core-stability muscles to

contract rapidly, just as they would in the movements involved in a boxing punch or a tennis serve.

Medicine balls come in different sizes, typically 1–10kg/2.2lb–22lb. Use the ball that matches your size and strength. Start with a lightweight ball and gradually progress to heavier ones when you feel ready.

For each exercise, take 2 to 3 seconds for each direction of the movement. Breathe out at the beginning of the movement, throughout the hold; breathe in as you return to the start position.

Slowly does it

It is important not to try to progress too fast with these exercises. First, master the basic and intermediate core exercises to take full advantage of what these medicine ball exercises have to offer, which will increase your heart rate by working many muscles simultaneously. Introduce the medicine ball gradually: try occasionally replacing one of your weekly cardiovascular sessions with a medicine ball core workout.

Medicine ball press-up

Muscles used Pectoralis major; rectus abdominis

Get into a press-up position, with one hand resting on the ball. Slowly lower your body, taking your elbows out to the side until they are at 90 degrees. Pause for a second, then return to the start position. As you get stronger, transfer more weight to the medicine ball side to make your stabilizing muscles work harder. Try taking one leg off the ground to make the exercise harder still. Begin with three sets of five repetitions, building up to five sets of twenty.

Single-leg squat to medicine ball shoulder press

Muscles used Gluteus medius; quadriceps; rectus abdominis

1 *Start by standing on one leg until your are balanced, with the other leg slightly bent, arms straight, holding the medicine ball above your head. Hold the ball still for a few seconds; this action will force the core muscles to tense involuntarily.*

2 *Bring the ball to chest height when you start squatting, to avoid putting pressure on the lower back. When the thigh of your squatting leg is parallel to the floor, pause, extend the leg and press the medicine ball above your head. Repeat with other leg. Do three sets of ten repetitions for each leg.*

Lunge with medicine ball; wood chop, high to low

Muscles used Obliques; gluteus – maximus and medius; quadriceps

1 *Stand with one foot in front of the other, about 60cm/2ft apart. Hold the medicine ball above your head with straight arms.*

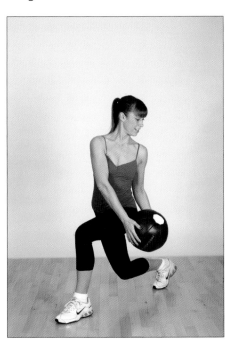

2 *Lunge and rotate your upper body across your front leg, lowering the ball until it is level with the hip. Pause for 1 second, then slowly return to the start position. Begin with three sets of five repetitions, then build up to three sets of ten repetitions.*

Medicine ball lunge with rotation

Muscles used Quadriceps; obliques – internal and external; gluteus medius

1 *Catch the medicine ball with your arms out in front of you. Keep yourself as stable as possible by tensing your core muscles to take the impact.*

3 *Turn back past the centre point and rotate your upper body out to the left. Focus on keeping your hips in line and stop the hips from rotating in the movement. Throughout the exercise, remember that it is the core muscles you are trying to work, so when they get tired, rest before your arms and back take over.*

2 *At the bottom of the lunge, turn your upper body to your right. Keep your arms straight throughout the rotation and maintain good shoulder posture.*

4 *When you come back up from the lunge, throw the ball back to your partner from chest height, keeping your core tense to give you a balanced base. To make this exercise harder, you can create more instability by placing your front foot on the flat surface of a BOSU. Begin with three sets of five repetitions, then build up to three sets of ten.*

Plyometrics Core Training

Plyometric exercises involve preloading a muscle and then aggressively leaping and bounding. They cause the neuromuscular system to respond faster and more powerfully than any other resistance or cardiovascular exercises.

Good core muscles are essential for plyometric exercises, which in turn are an advanced method of improving the strength of the core muscles. You need advanced core stability before you try plyometric exercises. If your core muscles are not strong, you will be prone to injury, and the power you generate with the leg muscles will be less effective.

Rapid response

Plyometrics refers to human movements that involve an eccentric (lengthening) muscle contraction followed immediately by a rapid concentric (shortening) muscle contraction. These types of training exercises are essential for fast sporting performance such as running, jumping and throwing. For example, a sprinter has their feet on the ground for less than 0.01 of a second so their muscles must respond to the rapid change in direction from when their foot strikes the ground to taking off again. A massive amount of force is required in a very short space of time. Plyometric exercises will not necessarily make you faster by enhancing your speed, but they will help to speed up the change in the period between a muscle lengthening and shortening. The phase between the muscle lengthening and shortening is called the amortization phase.

Preparation for plyometrics

You need to have a good base of strength training before you can do plyometrics. It would be advisable to be able to squat at least your body weight before you start plyometrics training. If your muscles are not strong enough you will be susceptible to injury. Plyometrics workouts should be classed in the same bracket as strength training workouts, in terms of the afterburn of calories. Endurance athletes will get little advantage from doing plyometrics. Your muscles will be broken down and therefore your body will take time to recover with an increase in calories used to make this recovery happen.

You should always have someone watching you in your first few weeks of plyometric workouts. It is easy to get the techniques wrong and this will seriously impinge on the effectiveness of the workouts. Neuromuscular pathways will be enhanced with plyometrics training if it is done correctly. Your neuromuscular system must be continually stimulated in anaerobic activities to make improvements in your sporting activity.

Lunge jump

Muscles used Quadriceps; gluteus medius

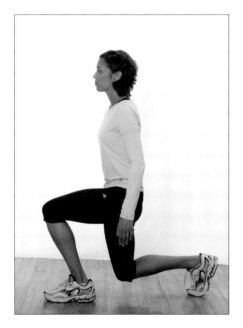

1 *Lunge down, with your left foot forward, and your arms hanging down by your sides. Keep your left knee just over the foot.*

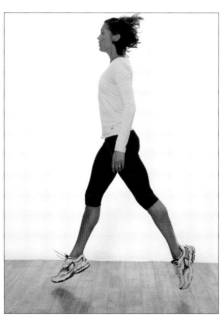

2 *Spring up into the air, at the same time changing over your legs so that you can land with your right foot in front.*

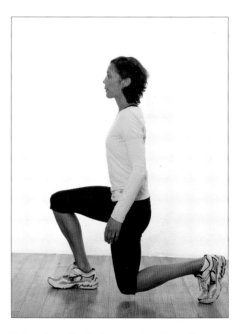

3 *Land on both feet, and soften the impact by bending your knees, arms still at your sides. Begin with three sets of four repetitions for each leg.*

Single-leg squat jump

This uses the same technique as the squat jump, but using one leg only. Your stabilizers have to work hard to prevent lateral movement and your leg takes double the normal force. Begin with three sets of five repetitions, and build up to three sets of ten repetitions.

Muscles used Quadriceps; gluteus medius

1 *Stand on one leg with the other leg trailing behind you and squat down. Move left arm forward for balance.*

2 *Straighten your leg as forcefully as possible to take off the ground using your arms to help to drive you upward.*

3 *Land softly on the same leg; bend at the knee on impact with the floor and push your hips back behind you.*

Lateral jump

Muscles used Quadriceps; gluteus medius

1 *From a squatting position, straighten up to extend your legs as fast as possible.*

2 *Jump up with a sideways movement over a box, with your arms held out at the sides.*

3 *Land on both feet, softening the impact by bending your knees. Begin with three sets of five repetitions.*

Getting it right

Teaching your body to use muscles in the wrong way will lead to poor muscle recruitment and a need to start all over again because neuromuscular pathways will not be working correctly. Therefore it is crucial to get these exercises right first time. To get the most out of this type of training leave at least two days between sessions and avoid any strength training in between. Make sure you are wearing the correct footwear for your plyometric workouts to give you adequate stability. Good quality running shoes will give you the support and cushioning you need.

Sport and weight loss

If you take time to do exercises in your training to advance your core stability, your body will become better equipped to cope with your chosen sporting activity. If you are trying to lose weight, plyometrics core training will challenge your body to work in a different way, making you burn more calories and increasing your lean muscle mass – just 20 minutes a week will be enough to reap the benefits and feel the difference. You should have at least two days' rest between plyometric exercise routines to allow your muscles and joints to recover fully.

Warm up well

Because a large amount of force is generated very quickly, for example when doing a jump, there is a lot of stress on joints and a possibility of injury to muscles and joints so any training session which includes plyometric exercises should include a good dynamic warm-up, designed if possible to suit your sport. Go through some of the plyometric exercises in slow motion to prepare your muscles for the movements. Your muscles will come under huge stress, so they need to feel warm and high in energy. Avoid doing this after strength or cardiovascular training.

Squat jump

Muscles used Quadriceps; gluteus maximus

1 *With your feet slightly apart and flat on the floor, bend your knees and squat down so that you feel stable and balanced, then push your hips backward. Straighten the arms and stretch them out behind you so that they are straight and parallel to the ground.*

2 *Quickly move your arms forward and stretch them out in front, so they are raised just above head height. Extend your legs as fast as you possibly can, then jump high into the air. For the maximum effect, you need to make the movement as quickly and as smoothly as possible.*

3 *Land on both feet, softening the impact by bending the knees until you are in the starting position. Pause for 1 second, then repeat. Try jumping forward across the room and see how far you are able to jump. Begin with three sets of five repetitions, building up to three sets of twenty repetitions.*

Squat throw

Muscles used Quadriceps; rectus abdominis

1 *Catch a medicine ball in front of your chest and squat down at the same time, pushing your hips back behind you. Focus on tensing your abdominals to keep a solid base.*

2 *As you extend your legs to stand back up, throw the medicine ball back to your training partner. Do the movement as fast as possible to make it more effective. Begin with three sets of five repetitions, building up to three sets of ten repetitions.*

Overhead slam

Muscles used Rectus abdominis; pectoralis major; latissimus dorsi; seratus anterior; triceps

1 *Stand with feet hip-width apart and hold the medicine ball above your head, tensing your core muscles.*

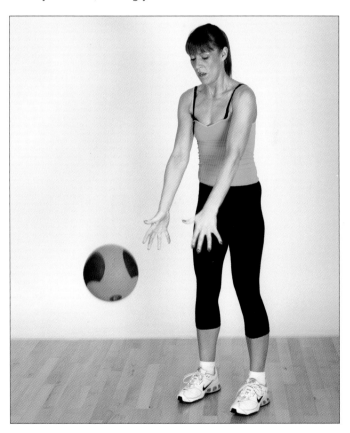

2 *Keeping your core tense, throw the medicine ball down in front of your feet as hard as possible and catch it on the rebound. Rest for 2 to 3 seconds after the first set, then repeat for three sets of five repetitions, building up to five sets of ten repetitions.*

Combining Core and Resistance Exercises

Once you have built up your core muscles, and you have confidence in your ability to recruit them for balance and stability, you can use them to help you perform a range of bigger exercises for increased muscle mass and greater strength.

Combining core and resistance exercises is the most advanced form of core-stability training. It is crucial that these exercises are not attempted until you have been through the process of beginner, intermediate and advanced core training. Once you have reached this stage, you will really begin to appreciate the benefits of your core strength when you are taking part in any of your sporting activities. Your body will subconsciously switch on the correct core muscles to help you to perform appropriately in any movement or exercise.

Squat to cable shoulder press

Muscles used Quadriceps; deltoids; gluteus maximus; rectus abdominis

1 This exercise is an efficient way of building power from your feet up toward your hands. Stand comfortably, with your feet hip-width apart. Holding the cables in both hands, squat down and pause for 1 second when your thighs are almost parallel with the floor.

2 Press the cables above your head, keeping your core tense. Try doing this exercise on one leg and using just one hand to make your core muscles work harder. Begin with three sets of five repetitions; build up to three sets of 15 to 20 repetitions.

Press-up to single-arm dumbbell row

Muscles used Gluteus medius; latissimus dorsi; obliques – internal and external

1 Adopt a press-up position, gripping one dumbbell in each hand. Lower your body toward the floor.

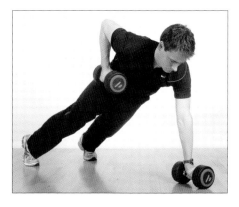

2 With the elbows at 90 degrees, pause for a second, then return to the start position, taking one dumbbell into the side of your ribs, your elbow brushing past your ribs and back behind you. Begin with three sets of three repetitions, building up to three sets of ten repetitions.

Single-leg squat to single-arm dumbbell row and frontal raise

Muscles used Quadriceps; gluteus maximus; deltoids; rectus abdominis

1 *Gripping a dumbbell in one hand, balance and squat down on one leg, then lift the other leg off the floor, and at the same time, pull the dumbbell in toward your ribs. Throughout the exercise, maintain a neutral spine to prevent your back muscles overworking.*

2 *Pause for a second, then, with a straight arm, raise your hand out in front of you to just above eye height. At the same time, straighten your leg. Make sure your belly button is sucked in all the time. Begin with three sets of three repetitions for each side of the body, building up to three sets of ten.*

Daily benefit

After doing these exercises, and when you find that you are able to do the maximum set of repetitions with ease, you will notice that your core muscles start to respond naturally to everyday actions such as bending down and twisting to pick something up from the floor.

The exercises will also provide you with the stability and focused training that you need for your chosen sport. You will find that actions such as hitting a golf ball, tackling your opposition to the ground in a rugby game or hitting a tennis serve, will become easier.

To benefit from these exercises, they do not have to take up an entire exercise session – you could simply include one or two advanced core exercises in each of your weekly training routines. This way, you won't get bored with your routines, and your core muscles will remain switched on throughout the rest of your cardiovascular or weight-training session.

Squat to cable rotation

Muscles used Quadriceps; gluteus medius; obliques – internal and external

1 *With the feet shoulder-width apart, grip the cable in both hands, squat down and rotate toward the machine, keeping your arms as straight as possible. Keep your legs bent in the squat.*

2 *Rotate across your body away from the machine. Pause, then return to a straight position. Keep your hips pushed back behind you to take the strain from your knees. Begin with three sets of four repetitions, build up to three sets of ten.*

TRAINING PLANS

Having established your goals, you need a training plan to achieve them, safely and effectively. Use the cardiovascular, strength, flexibility and core-stability tests described earlier in the book to assess your fitness levels. Then, decide what you want to concentrate on and devise an appropriate strategy. The following plans will help you to achieve goals such as gaining strength and losing weight, becoming a better runner and de-stressing. Remember, training with a partner will improve your technique and motivation. Before you begin, start your training diary.

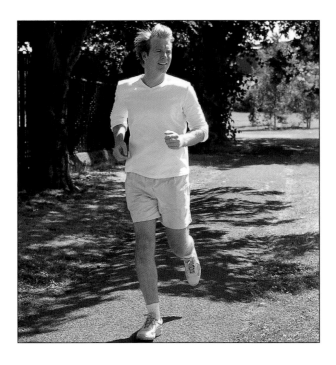

Above: Your exercise plan should contain different types of training to make it more challenging and fun.
Left: Once you have worked out what training to do, you will feel more motivated.

Weight-loss Plan

Losing weight is one of the most common goals of people who take up fitness training. Follow this plan for six weeks and you should see great results. Keep an accurate training diary, including a record of your body measurements, to monitor your progress.

In order to burn off fat, you need to make all your big muscles work hard to promote stronger muscles. They will then act as living tissue to burn off calories. Throughout your weight-loss workouts, try to keep your heart rate at Level 2–3, i.e. you should always be slightly out of breath. Resistance training will help to give you a faster-acting metabolism, so it should become a major part of your training. Always do resistance training to prevent further weight gain.

The importance of diet

In order to lose weight, exercise should go hand in hand with a low GI diet. Once you have established a good training pattern, focus on your nutrition, as this is the most important factor in a weight-loss programme.

Resistance is useful

You may burn more calories during a cardiovascular workout than a resistance training session, but the afterburn following a resistance training session is far greater. When your muscles are recovering, they will burn off additional

Above: Resistance exercises will help muscles burn up calories, resulting in weight loss.

Training strategies
- Resistance exercises should alternate between upper- and lower-body exercises, to allow your upper body to rest while at the same time your lower body is working, and vice versa.
- Remember to include some stretches in your warm-up routine, and also at the end of every session, to help you to stay flexible and avoid injury.
- Core-stability training is vital to help you to carry out the cardiovascular and resistance training correctly without injury, so include core-stability exercises at least once a week. Start with basic core exercises and, as you master the exercises, progress to the more advanced exercises.

---

calories. If you are very unfit, the chances are that you won't be able to manage more than 5 minutes of cardiovascular exercise because you will soon be uncomfortably out of breath. However, resistance training will not leave you as breathless, so it is an easier, as well as a more effective, method of

Below: The right diet, preferably a low GI diet, with exercise, are essential elements in a weight-loss programme.

Below: You don't have to go to the gym to lose weight, you can do certain exercises at home.

weight loss for the unfit person. Also, by beginning your weight-loss programme with basic resistance training, you soon gain greater strength in your muscles, which will help you to cope with longer cardiovascular sessions. Never underestimate the power of resistance training for weight loss.

Six-week weight-loss plan

As you get fitter, increase the intensity and duration of your cardiovascular exercises. You need continually to challenge your body to make it burn more calories so try doing intervals going from Level 2 (medium-intensity training) to Level 3 (high-intensity training) for up to 1 minute at a time. Take steps to stay motivated throughout your training. Consistency and regular training is the key to losing weight so pick a time to follow the plan when you will not be distracted by other events in your life. Follow this plan for six weeks to put you well on your way to significant weight loss. Be flexible – if you cannot cycle or run because of poor weather conditions, simply choose one of the other day's activities until you are able to get outside again. This weight-loss plan is suitable for men and women.

Day	Exercise	Time/Sets/Reps/Level	Comments
Monday	Rowing	5 minutes L1–L2	Warm up your muscles to reduce the risk of injury
	Leg press	3 x 20	Firms and strengthens calf muscles
	Olympic bar chest press	3 x 20	Tones and shapes the chest
	Cycling	5 minutes steady L2	Low-impact aerobic exercise that burns up calories
	Leg extension	3 x 20	Strengthens and works upper legs
	Dumbbell chest press	3 x 20	Intense workout of the upper arm, chest and shoulder
	Treadmill walk	5 minutes L2–L3	Use + 5 per cent incline
	Lunge	3 x 20	Works the upper leg and buttocks
	Lat pull-down	3 x 20	Trains the neglected back muscles
	Rowing machine	5 minutes L2	Cool down gives time to return the blood flow to normal
Tuesday	Basic core stability	Hold each exercise 20 seconds	Builds up the muscles of the trunk that control the spine
	Walking	20–40 minutes	Burn 300–400 calories per hour when walking briskly
Wednesday	Cycling	5 minutes L1–L2	Warm up and do stretches
	Step-up	3 x 20	Start with 3 x 10
	Bench press-up	3 x 10–20	Progress to full press-ups
	Treadmill walk/run	5 minutes L2–L3	Use +5 per cent incline
	Machine leg curls	3 x 20	Exercises the hamstrings
	Dumbbell flies	3 x 20	Works the middle of the chest
	Rowing	5 minutes L2–L3	Cardiovascular exercise works the upper body
	Side lunges	3 x 20	Work hips, buttocks and thighs
	Dumbbell shoulder press	3 x 15	For shoulder and upper-arm strength
	Cycling	5 minutes L2	Cool-down
Thursday	Basic core stability	2–3 seconds for each direction of the movement	Work all the major muscles in the trunk, try raises, planks, fit ball, BOSU and medicine ball exercises
	Walking	20–40 minutes	Option to run or bike
Friday	Treadmill walk/run	5 minutes L1–2	Warm up and do stretches
	Lunge	3 x 20	Works most of the muscles in the upper leg and calf
	Arnie shoulder press	3 x 15	Strengthens shoulders, upper arms and chest
	Rowing	5 minutes L2–L3	Try intervals of 1 minute easy and 30 seconds hard
	Squat	3 x 20	Works the quadriceps muscles in the upper leg
	Upright cable row	3 x 15	Strengthen neck and shoulders
	Cycling	5 minutes L2–L3	Medium- to high-intensity training
	Calf raise	3 x 20	Stretches out the calf muscles
	Triceps dip	3 x 10–20	Works the upper arm and chest muscles
	Treadmill walk/run	5 minutes L1–L2	Cool down
Saturday	Walking	1–2 hours L2	Low-impact exercise
	Or Running	1–2 hours L2	One of the best forms of cardiovascular exercise
	Or Cycling	1–2 hours L2	Aerobic exercise
Sunday	Rest day	24 hours	Eases and repairs sore muscles

Weight-gain Plan: Muscle

Gaining weight in the form of muscle is another popular fitness-training goal. It calls for a strict regime of heavy resistance training and good nutrition. It also means avoiding all cardiovascular training for at least the first six weeks.

The correct resistance training, with more sets but fewer repetitions of heavy weights, along with regular training will help break down muscles for the whole body. These muscles then grow back stronger and bigger.

If possible, always have a training partner with you to watch your technique. Good technique will help you to isolate the muscles that you want to work effectively. A training partner is also invaluable support when your muscles fatigue when training to failure.

You must train all of the major muscles in your body to get bigger. There is no point in training your upper-body muscles and not your legs, if you want your legs to be strong enough to support you and not be vulnerable to injury. Focus on the bigger muscles – chest, back and tops of the legs – rather than the small muscles – the biceps and triceps – which will not add much to your overall size.

The biggest first

Always plan your training session so that you exercise your biggest muscles first. Otherwise, the supporting smaller muscles will be too weak to help train your bigger muscles. For example, do dumbbell chest presses before triceps dips so that your triceps muscles are fresh enough to help in the dumbbell chest press. Once you have followed the plan for about six weeks, make adjustments to focus on the areas of your body in which you want to see more growth. For example, if you want bigger shoulders, do two shoulder sessions in the week instead of one.

More food, more muscle

In order to increase muscle mass, you will simply have to consume more calories. Include a selection of mainly low to medium GI foods in your diet

Above: Having a training partner to help you lift heavy weights can motivate you and make training safer.

and increase the protein content of your food to 40 per cent. If you find it hard to eat larger portions of food, particularly foods in the protein group, then supplement your meals with protein shakes and bars, and make sure that you eat something every three hours.

Left: While you are doing resistance training, increase the protein in your diet with eggs, fish, meat and nuts.

Measure up

Before you begin training to increase your weight by increasing muscle tissue, take measurements of your neck, shoulders, biceps, chest, waist, thighs and calves. This will enable you to monitor your progress and see changes in your body shape that will help to motivate you.

Six-week weight-gain plan

Day	Exercise	Time/Sets/Reps/Level	Comments
Monday	Rowing	5 minutes L1	Warm up to reduce risk of injury
	Olympic bar chest press incline	5 x 6–8	Do incline first to isolate the chest more
	Dumbbell chest press incline	5 x 6–8	Gives a workout of the chest and upper arms
	Olympic bar chest press	5 x 6–8	Tones and shapes the chest
	Dumbbell chest press	5 x 6–8	Intense workout of upper arm, chest and shoulder
	Cable flies flat bench	5 x 6–8	Workout for chest, back, shoulders and arms
	Press-up	5 x 6–8	Good for strengthening back, chest and arms
	Triceps cable push-down	5 x 6–8	Strengthens upper arms, shoulders, chest and back
	Triceps bench dips	5 x max reps	Works upper arm and chest muscles
Tuesday	Hack squat	5 x 8–10	Good for upper legs and buttocks
	Leg press	5 x 8–10	Strengthens and firms leg muscles
	Lunge	5 x 8–10	Hold dumbbells to make it harder
	Step-up	5 x 8–10	Go as slow as possible on the drop back down
	Leg extension	5 x 8–10	Strengthens and works upper legs
	Ab crunch	5 x 10	Hold weight above head
	Hanging leg raise with twist	5 x 8–10	Builds up the abdominal muscles
Wednesday	Overhand chin-up, wide grip	3 x max reps	When you can do 10 reps, add a weights belt
	Lat pull-down, overhand grip	5 x 6–8	Be careful not to use your lower back
	Lat pull-down, underarm grip	5 x 6–8	Helps to train the back muscles
	Seated cable row	5 x 6–8	Especially strengthens the middle back and forearms
	Bent-over barbell row	5 x 6–8	Generally strengthens the back
	Barbell bicep curl, narrow grip	5 x 6–8	Workout for the biceps
	Concentration curl	5 x 6–8	Exercises the biceps
Thursday	Row	5 minutes L1	Warm up
	Hanging leg raise	5 x 10	Start with 3 sets and build up to 5 sets
	Sit-up, with Russian twist	5 x 20	10 each side
	Crunch	5 x 20	Tones and strengthens the abdominal muscles
	Reverse crunch	5 x 20	Gives stronger and sleeker abdominal muscles
	Dumbbell side bend	5 x 20	10 each side
	High cable side bend	5 x 20	10 each side
Friday	Olympic bar shoulder press	5 x 6–8	Improves shoulder strength and muscle mass
	Dumbbell shoulder press	5 x 6–8	For shoulder and upper arm strength
	Cable shoulder press	5 x 6–8	Strengthens upper arms, improves general fitness
	Shrug	5 x 6–8	Helps the trapezius muscle to become stronger
	Bent-over cable lateral raise	5 x 6–8	On each arm
	Dumbbell frontal raise	5 x 6–8	On each arm
	Overhead triceps extension	5 x 6–8	Increases strength and flexibility of the triceps
	Triceps press-up	5 x 6–8	Use decline to make it harder as you get stronger
Saturday	Dead lift	5 x 8–10	Tones the lower body and legs
	Dumbbell squat	5 x 8–10	Tones buttocks, hips and thighs
	Cable bicep curl	5 x 6–8	Works the biceps
	Barbell curl, wide grip	5 x 6–8	Builds up the outer biceps
	Concentration curl	5 x 6–8	Exercises the biceps
	Hammer curl	5 x 6–8	Works biceps, good for wrist, hand or elbow injuries
	Oblique crunch	5 x 10	10 each side
	High cable side bend	5 x 10	Works the oblique muscles at the sides of the abdome
Sunday	Rest day	24 hours	Eases and repairs sore muscles

Six-pack Plan

Many men look in the mirror and dream of having a taut, well-defined six-pack. The truth is, though, that achieving the desired effect takes a combination of dedicated training and consistently good nutrition.

Your training plan should consist of a combination of cardiovascular and resistance training. The cardiovascular training will burn off calories and increase your aerobic fitness, making your body work more efficiently. At first, stick to Level 2 for cardiovascular exercise such as running. As you get fitter, include intervals that will have a similar effect on your muscles as weight-training, i.e. exercises that will result in significant afterburn. For example, run at Level 2 for 4 minutes, then run fast at Level 3–4 for 1 minute, repeating this pattern throughout the session.

Diet and resistance training

Resistance training will help to build and strengthen muscles, and increase your metabolism. There is a direct link between the benefits of resistance training and your diet, so you will need to adjust the combination of the two to suit your personal requirements. There is a very fine balance between eating enough to retain muscle – and in the

Below: Eat well and stick to the plan for six weeks to achieve your six-pack.

process maintaining a high metabolism – and cutting back on food in order to reduce your body fat. Don't make the mistake – as many people do – of eating significantly less, as this will only result in your muscles not having enough energy and your metabolism declining to the point where you start to deposit fat. It is important that you eat every three to four hours. Also, you should eat mainly low GI foods

Above: Don't always stick to a rigid routine; try to vary it, otherwise you will become bored with training.

and it is crucial that your diet consists of 40 per cent protein. If you find it hard to include larger portions of protein in your daily diet, then try supplementing your meals with protein shakes and bars, and make sure that you eat every three hours.

Major muscle workout

You need to work all the major muscles in your body, not just your abdominals, in order to achieve a six-pack. Your abdominal muscles are small, so exercising them in isolation will not increase your metabolism sufficiently to get rid of the layer of fat that lies on top of them. During every exercise, concentrate on tensing your abdominal muscles to make them work harder. For example, during a leg press, tense your abdominals until you can feel them working as hard as your legs. Don't neglect your diet, you need good nutrition as well as exercise.

Six-pack training plan

Day	Exercise	Time/Sets/Reps/Level	Comments
Monday	Rowing	5 minutes L1	Warm up
	Dumbbell squat	3 x 20	Tones buttocks, hips and thighs
	Lunge	3 x 20	Works upper legs and buttocks
	Overhand chin-up, wide grip	5 x max reps	When you can do 10 reps, add a weights belt
	Overhand lat pull-down, wide grip	5 x 12	Exercises the muscles of the back
	Olympic bar chest press incline	5 x 12	Develops the mass and strength of the pectorals
	Olympic bar chest press	5 x 12	Heavy resistance to train chest muscles
	Dumbbell bicep curl	5 x 12	Develops and tones the biceps
	Bicep hammer curl	5 x 12	Builds up biceps and forearm muscles
Tuesday	Running	45–60 minutes L2–L3	Option to use cross-trainer
	Rowing	10 minutes L2–L3	Works upper body
	Crunch	3 x 20	Build up to 5 sets, hold weights plates
	Hanging leg raise	3 x 10	Build up to 20 reps as you get stronger
	High rope crunch	3 x 20	Build up to 5 sets
Wednesday	Rowing	5 minutes L1	Warm up
	Leg press	3 x 20	Tones and strengthens calf muscles
	Leg extension	3 x 20	Works on the muscles of the upper legs
	Overhand chin-up, wide grip	3 x max reps	When you can do 10 reps, add a weights belt
	Seated cable row	5 x 12	Works on forearms and middle back
	Dumbbell chest press	5 x 12	Exercises upper arms, chest and shoulders
	Lying cable flies	5 x 12	Good workout for chest muscles
	Cable lat raise	5 x 12	Works out shoulder muscles
	Cable frontal raise	5 x 12	Works anterior deltoids (front of chest)
Thursday	Running	45–60 minutes L2–L3	Option to use cross-trainer or rowing machine
	Hanging leg raise with twist	3 x 10	Build up to 5 sets
	Sit-up with Russian twist	3 x 20	Build up to 5 sets, use weights to make it harder
	Oblique crunch	3 x 20	Build up to 5 sets
	High rope crunch with twist	3 x 20	Build up to 5 sets
	Dumbbell side bend	3 x 20	Build up to 5 sets
	Side crunches	3 x 20	Build up to 5 sets
Friday	Rowing	5 minutes L1	Warm up
	Lunge	3 x 20	Works the upper leg and buttocks
	Machine leg curl	3 x 20	Develops hamstrings
	Dumbbell shoulder press	5 x 12	Strengthens shoulders and upper arms
	Upright row	5 x 12	Targets shoulders, upper back and biceps
	Dumbbell lat raises	5 x 12	Works upper chest
	Dumbbell frontal raises	5 x 10	10 each arm
	Triceps cable push-down	5 x 12	Develops triceps
	Bench triceps dip	3 x max reps	Strengthens triceps
Saturday	Running	45–60 minutes L2–L3	Option to use cross-trainer or rowing machine
	Crunch	3 x 20	Build up to 5 sets, hold weights above head to make it harder
	V-crunch	3 x 20	Build up to 5 sets
	Broomstick twist	3 x 20	Build up to 5 sets
	Kneeling cable rotation	3 x 20	Build up to 5 sets
	Dumbbell side bend	3 x 20	Build up to 5 sets
Sunday	Rest day	24 hours	Eases and repairs sore muscles

Wedding Dress Plan

On a day as important as your wedding, you will want to do yourself justice and look at your best. This workout will improve your shape and leave you feeling fit and toned for one of the most important days of your life.

This training plan will improve the parts of your body that will be most on show, or accentuated, when you are wearing your wedding dress: the buttocks, hips, underarms, abdominals, top of the chest and back of the arms.

If your wedding preparations run true to the norm, you can expect to lose some weight with the stress of it all in the last few weeks before the big day. This, combined with your workout sessions – which will also result in changes to your body shape – means that you need to be careful that your wedding dress is not suddenly a size too large. Aim to have achieved your desired shape before your last wedding-dress fitting.

Combination training

This workout plan combines a mixture of cardiovascular and resistance training. The cardiovascular training will increase your aerobic fitness, burn off calories,

Below: If you have stuck to the training plan, you should be happy with your appearance on your wedding day.

make your body work more efficiently and increase your energy levels. The resistance-training exercises will work big muscle groups to burn maximum calories and tone smaller muscles, such as your arms, to give you the look you want on the day. If you feel there are some parts of your body that need improving, focus your workouts on those areas and adjust the planned sessions to allow you to work on those areas two or three times a week for

Above: You will have your wedding photographs forever, so make sure that you look as good as you can.

Below: The fitter you are, the better you will be able to cope with the pressure on your big day.

Exercise tips

To get the best results from these exercises, make sure to eat healthily every three to four hours, consuming low GI foods, which will help your muscles to recover from exercise and maintain your energy levels.

Warm up for 5 to 10 minutes at Level 1 to Level 2 at the start of every training session, and complete stretches on the parts of your body that you will be using. Do a series of stretches again at the end of the workout.

faster results. Include core-stability training at least one day a week to help avoid injury and give you great posture. Start with the basic core exercises and progress onto the more advanced core exercises as you master them. Follow the plan for six weeks for great results.

Right: Basic core exercises will help to improve your posture and figure and get you into good shape.

Six-week wedding-dress plan

Follow this six-week plan and you will be feeling and looking great for your big day – and in the photographs afterward.

Day	Exercise	Time/Sets/Reps/Level	Comments
Monday	Cycling/running/cross-trainer	20–40 minutes L2	Use one or a combination
	Lunge	3 x 20	10 each leg; use dumbbells to make it harder
	Cable lat pull-down	3 x 20	Works back muscles and biceps
	Leg extension	3 x 20	Tones and works upper legs
	Dumbbell chest press	3 x 20	Isolates and works upper chest
	Incline bench	3 x 15	Strengthens and tones abdominal muscles
	Crunch	3 x 10	Start with 10 reps and build up to 20
	Bench triceps dip	3 x 10–20	Use straight legs to make it harder
Tuesday	Cycling/running/cross trainer	10–20 minutes L2	Use one or a combination
	Leg press	3 x 20	Tones and strengthens leg muscles
	Single-arm dumbbell row	3 x 15	Workout for the middle back muscles
	Leg curl	3 x 20	Exercises the hamstrings
	Dumbbell flies	3 x 15	Workout for the middle of the chest
	Oblique crunch	3 x 20	Works upper abdominals and obliques
	Dumbbell lat raise	3 x 15	Exercises the shoulders
Wednesday	Cycling/running/cross trainer	40–60 minutes L2–L3	2 minutes L3–4, alternating with 3 minutes L2
Thursday	Cycling	10 minutes L2	Warm up
	Bench drop lunge	3 x 20	10 each leg; use dumbbells to make it harder
	Single-leg hip raise	3 x 10	Workout for the buttocks
	Single-arm cable pull down	3 x 15	Mainly works lats, also biceps, middle back
	Bench press up	3 x 10–20	Works large muscles in the chest, also triceps
	Broomstick twist	3 x 20	Works obliques: the muscles at the side of abdomen
	Triceps cable push-down	3 x 15	Strengthens upper arms, shoulders, chest and back
Friday	Cycling/running/cross-trainer	10–20 minutes L2	Use one or a combination
	Side lunges	3 x 20	10 to each side to strengthen leg muscles
	Bent-over barbell row	3 x 15	Workout for the back
	Dumbbell flies	3 x 15	Exercise muscles at front of chest
	Cable adductors	3 x 20	10 each leg
	Plank	30–60-second hold	Builds endurance in abdominals and back
	Dumbbell bicep curl	3 x 15	Tones and strengthens biceps
Saturday	Cycling/running/cross trainer	40–60 minutes L2–L3	2 minutes L3–4, alternating with 3 minutes L2
Sunday	Rest day	24 hours	Eases and repairs sore muscles

Pregnancy Training Plan

Pregnancy is a very demanding time physically and mentally. However, by following the right exercise plan until late pregnancy, when you may find exercise uncomfortable, you can maintain your weight, reduce labour time, and make delivery easier.

Many women are understandably anxious about exercising when pregnant, but you can safely do a number of different types of exercise. Resistance exercises will make you stronger and less prone to injuries through overuse injuries as your baby gets bigger.

Basic core exercises will keep your spine and pelvis in line and prevent backache, while pelvic floor exercises will prevent incontinence. Regular exercise will increase your energy levels, improve self-esteem, help you to sleep better and enable you to get fitter after childbirth.

Pilates is a good way to increase the strength of your pelvic floor, support your back and position the baby for birth. Yoga will maintain muscle tone without impact. Swimming is one of the safest and most effective forms of exercise, as it works all the major muscles without any impact.

Below: Learn which exercises are appropriate so that you protect your unborn baby at all times.

Pregnancy training plan

Combine three daily sessions of pelvic floor exercises with weekly cardiovascular exercise – consisting of three 15–30-minute sessions – and two weekly resistance-training sessions.

Resistance training

Exercise	Time/Sets/Reps/Level	Comments
Walking/running or cross-trainer	5–10 minutes L1–L2	Warm up or cycle
Seated cable row	3 x 10–12	Works back and forearms
Leg extension	3 x 10–12	Tones upper legs
Dumbbell chest press incline	3 x 10–12	Works chest and arms
Lat pull-down	3 x 10–12	Works back muscles
Seated leg curl	3 x 10–12	Exercises hamstrings
Dumbbell fly	3 x 10–12	Works middle of the chest
Dumbbell lat raise	3 x 10–12	Exercises the shoulders
Dumbbell bicep curl	3 x 10–12	Strengthens biceps
Bench triceps dip	3 x 10–12	Strengthens triceps

Cardiovascular training

Exercise	Time/Sets/Reps/Level	Comments
Option 1: Stationary bike	10–20 minutes L1–L2	If you cannot hold a conversation, then you are going too fast
Option2: Treadmill walk/run	10–20 minutes L1–L2	Use without incline
Option 3: Cross-trainer	10–20 minutes L1–L2	Use for warm-up
Pelvic floor exercises	5–10 seconds	Stand, lie down or sit

Watchpoints

Seek advice from a midwife or doctor before you start any exercise plan, particularly if your pre-pregnancy body mass index (BMI) was over 35. While you should be keeping fit during pregnancy, this is not the time to make dramatic improvements in your fitness. Instead, aim to maintain the fitness you had before you became pregnant. Your exercise should not be above Level 2 if you are of average fitness, and no higher than Level 3 if you are above average fitness. If you cannot hold a conversation while exercising, you are training too hard.

Because of the extra weight you are carrying, you should avoid exercises with lots of impact in the third trimester.

As it is vital to minimize the risk of loss of balance and foetal trauma throughout pregnancy, you should definitely not undertake sports such as horse-riding, skiing, cycling, ice-skating and scuba diving.

Looser joints Be aware that during pregnancy a hormone called relaxin is released into the body. This hormone helps your joints to loosen in preparation

Warning

Stop exercising immediately if you feel any chest pain, headaches, dizziness, swelling, overtiredness, abdominal pain, nausea, dizziness, pelvic pain, contractions or lack of foetal movement.

Above: If you feel tired, stop training and take a rest. Don't push yourself if you don't feel like exercising.

for childbirth, but it also means that some exercises should be avoided: lunges, deep squats, step-ups and full sit-ups may damage the pelvic floor.

Relaxin, which is a hormone that relaxes the pelvic ligaments, may also affect other joints, particularly the wrists, elbows and knees, so use only light weights and do no more than 12 repetitions. Listen to your body and make sure you are comfortable during training.

Heat, hydration and hypoglycaemia
Avoid getting too hot by not exercising in hot or humid conditions and wearing the correct clothing. Stay well hydrated to keep your body temperature normal. Eat plenty before and after exercise to prevent hypoglycaemia (low blood-sugar levels) and do not exercise for more than 40 minutes.

The importance of position In the second and third trimester, the pressure of the baby on your blood vessels may cause blood to pool in your legs, so sit

down for resistance exercises and do not do any exercises involving movements above your head. Similarly, do not exercise lying on your back, as the pressure of the baby can cause low blood pressure.

Pelvic floor exercises
The easiest way to locate your pelvic floor muscles is by closing and pulling in both the front and back passages as if you were stopping yourself from urinating and defecating. Then, contract the muscles for 5 seconds to begin with, building up at your own pace to more than 10 seconds. If you struggle to achieve this when standing, try contracting your muscles when lying down, then progress to sitting up and, finally, standing.

Pelvic lift

1 *Lie on your back, bend your knees and plant your feet on the floor more than hip-width apart. Turn your toes slightly inward to engage the muscles of the inner thighs and groin area. Put palms down on the floor and breathe in.*

2 *Tense your buttocks and lift your hips off the floor. Hold for 5 seconds. Repeat ten times.*

Side stretch to alleviate heartburn

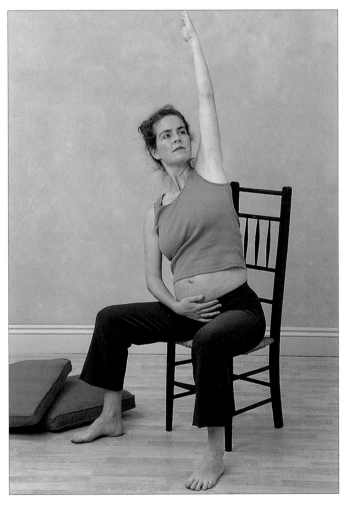

Sit on a firm chair with knees wide and feet flat on the floor. Bring your left arm out to the side and up overhead, stretching your left side. Look up at your hand, breathe deeply and hold the position. Repeat on the other side.

Postnatal Training Plan

Postnatal exercise is the best way to get back in shape and improve your self-esteem. A combination of cardiovascular and resistance training will help you to lose weight, increase your energy levels and help you cope with the emotional ups and downs.

If you feel comfortable and have had a normal birth, you can start to do some light exercise as soon as possible afterward. However, it is normal to wait for six to eight weeks before making dramatic improvements to your fitness level. During this time, you should avoid any high-impact training. Always seek advice from your doctor about the best time to start exercising.

If you have had a caesarean, you must get your doctor's approval before you begin any training. As it normally takes six to eight weeks before you are ready to begin any form of exercise, there is no point rushing to regain your pre-pregnancy fitness level. Your body has undergone major physical changes, so take your time, be patient and concentrate on your core muscles and pelvic floor strength.

What to avoid

It is important to check that your abdominal muscles have returned to normal, as they can get overstretched during pregnancy (diastasis rectus abdominis). To check the state of your abdominal muscles, lie down, then place your hand, palm down, just above your belly button, with your fingers pointing down toward your pubic bone. Try to lift your head and shoulders off the floor by tensing your abdominal muscles. You should feel them coming together. If you don't feel the abdominals

working, you should begin with pelvic floor exercises described in the pregnancy training plan and avoid doing sit-ups until you can feel your abdominals working correctly.

Your joints and ligaments will still be loose after the birth, so avoid any exercises involving significant impact or exercises such as lunges, squats, step-ups and hip adduction/abduction until you feel you have full control. Use light weights only and do no more than 12 repetitions during any session.

Above: Increase your fitness and strength, and get back into shape, while your baby is growing.

Building fitness

Start your cardiovascular fitness by walking at least three times a week for 15 minutes, building up to 30 minutes. If walking feels uncomfortable, then use the bike or do cross-trainer exercises instead. Include the pelvic floor in your training every day. You can start doing some pelvic floor squeezes the day after childbirth, if it was an easy delivery.

Postnatal exercise plan

If you apply yourself to this daily routine following childbirth, you will soon be able to resume your normal fitness training.

Exercise	Time/Sets/Reps	Comments
Pelvic tilt	10 x 10 seconds	Begin with 5 seconds and build up to 10 seconds
Pelvic floor squeeze	10 x 10 seconds	At least 4 x daily
Transverse abdominal	10 x 10 seconds	Begin with 5 seconds and build up to 10 seconds
Half crunch	3 x 10–20	Avoid tensing your neck
Reverse crunch	3 x 10–20	Keep your lower back pushed into the floor

Calories for energy
If you are breastfeeding your baby, make sure that you eat sufficient calories to enable you to have enough energy to exercise and recover. Eat low-to-medium GI foods to give you long-lasting energy.

Begin by contracting the pelvic floor for 5 seconds, and building up to 10 seconds after a few days. Once you feel ready, you can attempt faster contractions, with up to 10 every 30 seconds.

Introduce abdominal exercises as soon as you feel comfortable enough to do so, and you have had the go-ahead from your doctor. Start resistance training once your pelvic floor and abdominals are strong enough to support you in the exercises you want to do. Use the same resistance exercises that you did while pregnant before moving on to a more advanced training plan of your choice.

Below: Make sure you are fit enough to cope with the physical demands of a lively, active child.

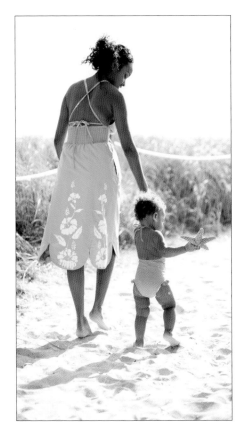

Exercises to relieve tension in the back: floor twist

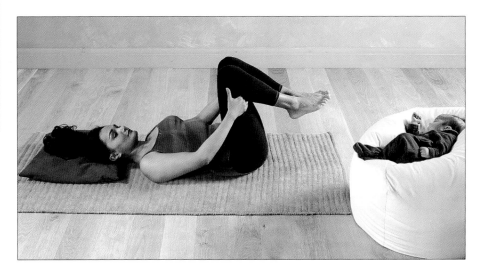

1 *Lie on your back, contract your pelvic floor, tense your abdominals and draw your knees toward your chest. Repeat a few times to loosen up the lower and middle back.*

2 *Extend left arm along floor, breathe in and drop your bent legs to the right with your right hand supporting them. To make the twist stronger, turn head to the left.*

3 *Breathe in to bring the legs back to the start position over your chest, using your right hand to help lift their weight. Repeat the movement to the left and continue several times on each side. Relax with your knees bent to finish.*

Older Person's Plan

Your metabolism declines with age, so it is vital to eat healthily and take regular exercise to maintain your muscles. If you are exercising for the first time since your youth, take any exercise slowly and seek advice from your doctor before you start.

Because your metabolic rate declines after the age of 30, you need to boost it by doing resistance exercises, that is, you apply resistance to a particular movement. This type of exercise will give you greater strength and energy and the afterburn continues to use up calories long after your training session is over.

When you are doing resistance exercises, avoid overhead exercises and those that involve keeping your balance. Listen to your body and stop well before training to failure, which could cause injury, and is unnecessary. Don't exercise beyond Level 3 (*see* page 41) during the cardiovascular exercises; you should still be able to easily hold a full conversation.

Have a training partner with you to help you to set up the weights and be on hand to assist, should you need it. If you are unsure about any exercises in the gym, ask an instructor to help you.

Below: Maintaining your fitness levels as you get older will help to improve the quality of your life.

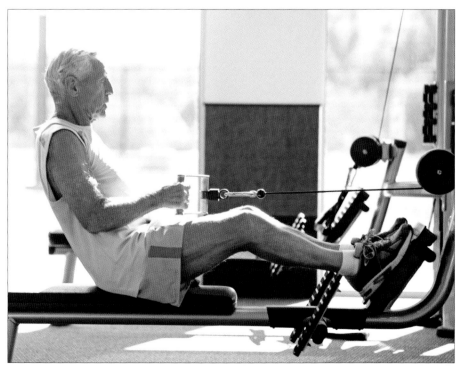

Above: If you are unsure about what type of exercise you should do, seek help from an expert.

Breathing exercises

To avoid a rise in blood pressure, use the breathing exercises, especially when doing resistance exercises. Working with the wrong weights can lead to a rise in blood pressure, so make sure that you use weights that are light enough for you to do at least 15 repetitions.

Exercises for strong bones

To avoid osteoporosis, include impact exercises, such as step-ups and walking. Do not move too quickly after leg exercises, as it will take some time for the blood to be redistributed through the body.

Exercise sessions to maintain strength and flexibility

Attempt to do each session once a week. Use the first 5 minutes of each session to get warmed up. As well as these sessions, continue to exercise out of the gym with walks of varying pace and terrain.

Session	Exercise	Time/Sets/Reps/Level	Comments
One	Cycling	5–10 minutes L1–L2	Use as warm-up
	Leg extension	3 x 15–20	Strengthens and tones upper legs
	Standing squat	3 x 15–20	Don't let your knees go forward of your feet; use dumbbells to make it harder
	Overhand cable lat pull-down, wide grip	3 x 15–20	Works back muscles and biceps
	Dumbbell chest press	3 x 15–20	Works upper arms, chest and shoulders
	Incline bench	3 x 15	Strengthens and tones abdominal muscles
	Cable triceps push-down	3 x 15–20	Exercises triceps
	Treadmill walk	5–10 minutes L2–3	Use incline to make it harder
Two	Treadmill	5–10 minutes L1–L2	Builds general fitness and stamina
	Seated leg curl	3 x 15–20	Tones up back of upper thighs
	Hip raises	3 x 15–20	Progress to single-leg hip raises
	Single-arm cable pull-down	3 x 15–20	Works lats, also biceps and middle back
	Dumbbell fly	3 x 15–20	Works the middle of the chest
	Dumbbell bicep curl	3 x 15–20	Optimum workout for the biceps
	Cycling	5–10 minutes L1–L2	Warm down
Three	Rowing	5–10 minutes L1–L2	Use correct technique to avoid injury
	Step-up small step aerobics step	3 x 15–20	Exercises and tones leg muscles
	Dumbbell side bends	3 x 15–20	Works obliques and abdominal muscles
	Straight arm cable pull-down	3 x 15–20	Exercises the back muscles and the triceps
	Knee press-up	3 x 5–10	Progress to bench press-ups, then full press-ups when you feel ready
	Dumbbell lat raise	3 x 10–15	Works the deltoid muscles
	Cycling	5–10 minutes L1–L2	Use to warm down

Above: Resistance training is the key to maintaining your muscles as you age.

Core-stability exercises

Include some basic core-stability exercises once a week for good posture and to hold your spine and pelvis in place. Start with basic core exercises, such as a plank, side plank raise, plank to single-leg raise and single-leg stand, and gradually progress to the more advanced levels.

Nutrition

It is very important that you plan a healthy diet and eat low GI foods in order to maintain your energy levels, and eat every three to four hours to keep your metabolism high and prevent weight gain.

If you feel very tired or faint during training, eat high GI foods, which will result in a rapid increase in your blood sugar level.

Make sure also that you have a diet that is high in protein to maintain muscle strength and to help them recover from your workouts. Remember – the more muscle you have, the more active your metabolism will become.

Right: Your exercise will be more enjoyable if you share the activity with someone else.

De-stress Plan

You may think that you are simply too busy to exercise or too exhausted to find the motivation. But the less exercise you do, the less energy you have, so take what little time you have, get to the gym and use this plan to improve your overall fitness.

A regular exercise plan will give you the energy you need to take on everyday challenges. While you are exercising, you should concentrate on the task in hand, which should prevent you from dwelling on other stresses in your life.

Try the two sessions of the de-stress plan and in between the sessions, do some cardiovascular training for 20–40 minutes, such as running, rowing, cycling and cross-trainer exercises. These sessions should be at a level where you start to feel out of breath. Spend most of your cardiovascular session in Level 2 and include up to 10 x 1-minute efforts at Level 3 to further increase your heart rate and improve your recovery rate. Having these 1-minute efforts to concentrate on will focus your mind fully on the exercise. You could make these 1-minute efforts shorter but increase the intensity to work at Level 4.

Rest between your efforts needs to last long enough for you to recover enough to tackle the next effort. Start with 3 minutes between each effort and

Above: Try interval training to make best use of your exercise session. This is riding fast for 1–10 minutes, resting to recover, then repeating a few times.

Left: Stress at work can be managed by exercising to increase energy levels.

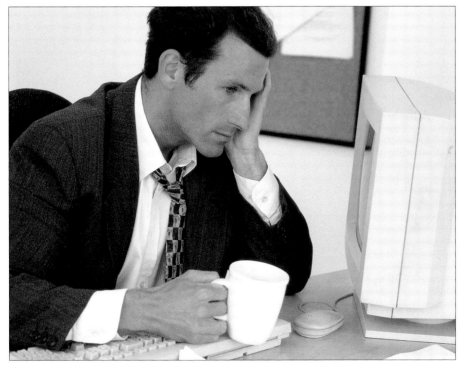

Increasing weights
For the resistance exercises, pick a weight that you can comfortably use for the time allocated for each exercise. If you are using dumbbells, have a range of weights close by so that you can quickly switch weights to make the exercise easier or more difficult. As you increase in strength, you will be able to gradually increase the weight that you can lift.

drop it to 90 seconds when you feel fit enough. It is hard to motivate yourself to exercise when you are stressed from a day's work so set yourself targets in your workouts. Aim to lift a bigger weight or run farther in a certain time. You must also keep your exercise as regular as possible so you keep up a level of fitness that enables you to feel good when you exercise rather than wishing you hadn't let your fitness slip away from you.

Nutrition

It is important to eat healthily if you have a busy life. If you spend 10 minutes a day making healthy food, you will find everyday tasks easier, and your energy levels will remain constant, so you can fit more into your day. Stick to eating low to medium GI foods and stay hydrated. Alcohol will not help you to de-stress – it will only make you more tired and even less inclined to exercise.

Releasing tension

Boxercise is one of the best ways to de-stress, so if you have a training partner who will hold the pads for you, go for it. Begin with 5 minutes at a time, building up to around 15 minutes. Try doing a boxercise session in place of some of the cardiovascular exercises in your training week.

Below: A boxing session is a great way to unwind and get rid of stress.

De-stress exercise plan

Take 10 to 20 seconds' rest between each exercise to allow your body to recover just enough to complete the next set without your heart rate going down. To make your de-stress plan complete, include at least one session of core-stability exercises, starting at the basic level and working up through the levels, to improve your posture and prevent injuries such as back pain in everyday movements or through too much time spent being sedentary.

Make sure you warm up for 5 to 10 minutes at Level 1 to Level 2, then spend 5 minutes stretching to prepare your muscles for the workout. Try to do at least two workouts a week.

Session	Exercise	Time/Level	Comments
One	Cycling	5 minutes L1–L2	Warm up
	Treadmill	5–10 minutes L2–L3	Builds fitness
	Overhand lat pull-down, wide grip	30 seconds	Works back
	Step-up	60 seconds	30 seconds on each leg
	Press-up	30 seconds	Build up to 60 seconds
	Single-arm dumbbell row	60 seconds	30 seconds on each arm
	Lunge	60 seconds	30 seconds on each leg
	Dumbbell chest press incline	30 seconds	Increase weight as strength increases
	Rowing	5 minutes L3–L4	Go as far as possible
	Dumbbell shoulder press	30 seconds	Works shoulders
	Dumbbell squat	60 seconds	Works buttocks
	Bench triceps dip	30 seconds	Build up to 60 seconds
	Crunch	60 seconds	Tones abdominals
	Treadmill walk/run	5 minutes L2–L3	For stamina
	Warm down	5 minutes	Stretches
Two	Cycling	5 minutes L1–L2	Warm up
	Rowing	5–10 minutes L2–L3	Works upper body
	Bent-over barbell row	30 seconds	Works back muscles
	Side lunge	60 seconds	Strengthens legs
	Dumbbell chest press	30 seconds	Works chest, arms
	Single-arm cable pull-down	60 seconds	30 seconds on each arm
	Side step-up	60 seconds	30 seconds on each leg
	Press-up	30 seconds	Works upper body
	Treadmill walk/run	5–10 minutes L2–L3	Builds stamina
	Arnie shoulder press	30 seconds	Works deltoids
	Calf raise	60 seconds	Works calf muscles
	Dumbbell bicep curl	30 seconds	Works the biceps
	Sit-up with Russian twist	30 seconds	Build up to 60 seconds
	Rowing	5 minutes L2–L3	Works upper body
	Warm down	5 minutes	Stretches

Outdoor Training Plan

For people who find gyms intimidating or just plain inconvenient, the following outdoor programmes are ideal, especially in a park where you can use benches and trees in place of gym equipment.

If you like to walk or jog with a partner, it is not always possible to match your running pace, which can leave both of you frustrated. The faster person wants to go faster, and the slower person feels they are letting their training partner down by slowing them up. By introducing the approach to training outlined here, the fitter person can follow these exercise plans while waiting for their partner to catch up.

Build up strength

For the first two weeks, do 20 seconds of each exercise, building up to 40 seconds and then 60 seconds once you are confident of your strength. Jog or walk between the exercises to keep your heart rate at Level 2 to Level 3. If you would prefer to walk rather than run, use fast walking to keep your heart rate high, and include some hills to make the session more beneficial.

Below: Running outside in the fresh air is exhilarating, and gives you the chance to explore new places.

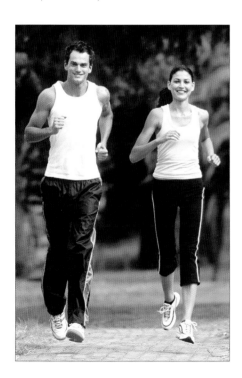

Outdoor exercise plan

Each session is only about 30 minutes long; do session one and two each week, on different days, and after just three to four weeks of training you will notice how much easier they are. Your recovery rate between exercises will also have improved dramatically.

Session	Exercise	Time/Sets/Reps/Level	Comments
One	Walking/jogging	5 minutes L1–L2	Warm up
	Running	5 minutes L2–L3	Cardiovascular exercise
	Lunge	60 seconds	30 seconds on each leg
	Running	2 minutes L2–L3	Good for general fitness
	Bench step-up	60 seconds	30 seconds on each leg; use a park bench
	Running	2 minutes L2–L3	
	Bench press-up	60 seconds	Begin with 30 seconds; build up to 60 seconds
	Running	2 minutes L3–L4	
	Side lunge	60 seconds	30 seconds on each side
	Running	2 minutes L3–L4	
	Bench triceps dip	60 seconds	Works upper arms and chest
	Running	5–10 minutes L2–L4	Include 5 x 30-second hill runs at L4
Two	Walking/jogging	5 minutes L1–L2	Warm up
	Running	5 minutes L2–L3	
	Standing squat	60 seconds	Strengthens lower body
	Running	2 minutes L2–L3	
	Side step-up	60 seconds	Use park bench
	Running	2 minutes L2–L3	
	Bench drop lunge	60 seconds	Use park bench
	Running	2 minutes L3–L4	
	Triceps press-up	60 seconds	Use park bench; begin with 30 seconds; build up to 60 seconds
	Running	2 minutes L3–L4	
	Calf raise	60 seconds	Lean against back of park bench or tree
	Running	5–10 minutes L2–L4	Include 5 x 30-second sprints at L4

At the start of your workout, do your normal stretches using a park bench, which you can hold on to, lean against or place your leg on. Remember that core-stability training still needs to be part of your routine. If the ground is dry, do core exercises outside; if it is wet, do them in the comfort of your home. Try to include some core exercises at least once a week, beginning with the basic exercises and gradually progressing to the intermediate and more advanced exercises when you feel able to.

Bench step-ups

These can be done as part of a circuit or added to a running or walking session.

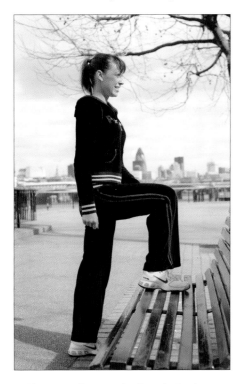

1 *Place one foot on the bench. Push up using the muscles in your front leg to lift you up so that both legs are standing on the bench.*

2 *Once you are standing upright on the bench, slowly lower yourself back to the ground using one leg at a time. Repeat using the other leg to start.*

Bench press-ups

Outdoor benches in parks or urban streets are ideal for doing press-ups since they are at a perfect height for these types of exercises.

1 *Start the press-ups by lowering yourself to the plank position with hands on the bench and elbows bent at 90 degrees.*

2 *Press up carefully until your arms are straight, then pause for a second before slowly lowering yourself back down to the start position.*

Bench triceps dips

Outdoor benches are normally the perfect height for triceps dips.

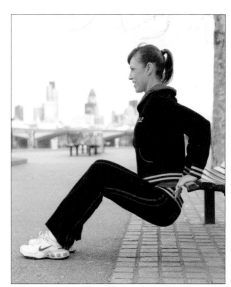

1 *Start by getting to the plank position with hands on the bench, fingers facing outward and your elbows bent at 90 degrees. Lower yourself so that your knees are bent and your feet are flat on the ground in front of you.*

2 *Once you have lowered yourself down, hold the position for a short time, then carefully begin to press back up to the straight arm starting position. Have a rest, then repeat the exercise. If your arms feel stiff, rub or shake them.*

Clothing

Wear several layers of clothing so that you can easily take them off if you get hot and maintain your body temperature at a comfortable level.

Precaution

Always carry a water bottle so that you can stay hydrated, and a mobile phone in case you have an injury or other emergency.

Travel Plan

When you are away from home, it is not always easy to get to the gym – which can be the perfect excuse to stop your fitness training. However, with the following plan, you have no reason to stop exercising.

This plan is designed for the traveller who has a limited amount of space in which to exercise, such as a hotel room, and no equipment to hand. For weights, you can improvise by using bottles of water. To support your back while doing floor exercises, use a blanket or folded towel. Remember – being on holiday is no excuse not to keep up with your exercise programme.

If you are staying at a hotel that offers the use of a gym to its guests, you just need the motivation to go every morning before you get involved in other activities. Having a gym so close at hand may even improve your fitness levels. And if the hotel does not have a gym, follow the traveller's fitness plan whenever you have a spare 20 minutes and you will feel the benefits.

The training sessions will keep your heart rate up and give your muscles a good workout. For maximum benefit, allow only 10–20 seconds between each exercise. If you want to keep your heart rate up during the session, you can also include marching or jogging on the spot between each exercise.

Improvised exercises

Above: Even if you have only a limited space, there is usually enough room to stretch so you can stay flexible.

Above: If you don't have suitable weights, simply use water bottles to do some lat raises.

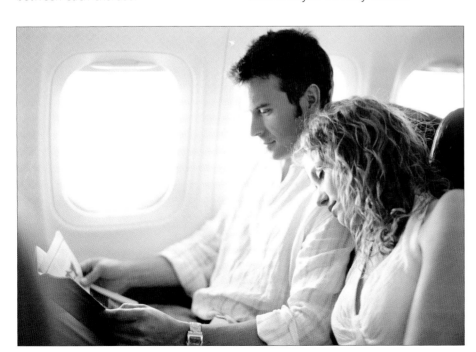

Travel tips

Include some basic core exercises every other day to keep your trunk muscles working well, especially if you are spending a significant amount of time sitting down.

Stretch after your warm-up, and also at the end of each session, to prevent your muscles from shortening during periods of travel.

Left: Even though you are immobile when you are travelling, it can still be a tiring process. It is therefore important to keep up your exercise wherever and whenever you can, so that you can maintain your energy levels.

Traveller's exercise plan

Each session should only take about 15 minutes, and you should always start with a good 5 minutes' warm-up at Level 1 to Level 2, followed by some stretches for the muscles you are going to use. Do just one or all the sessions when they fit into your schedule.

Session	Exercise	Time/Sets/Reps/Level	Comments
One	Walking, marching on spot	5 minutes L1–L2	Warm up
	Standing squat	60 seconds	Use water bottles as weights
	Press-up	30 seconds	Build up to 60 seconds
	Crunch	60 seconds	Exercises abdominal muscles
	Calf raises	60 seconds	Lean against the wall or door
	Body weight shoulder press	30 seconds	Strengthens shoulder muscles
	Oblique crunch	60 seconds	Works oblique abdominal muscles
	Frontal raises	60 seconds	30 seconds each arm, use water bottles as weights
	Hip raise	60 seconds	Strengthens buttock muscles
	Triceps dip	30 seconds	Build up to 60 seconds
Two	Walking, marching on spot	5 minutes L1–L2	Warm up
	Lunge	60 seconds	30 seconds on each leg
	V-crunch	30 seconds	Build up to 60 seconds
	Single-leg squat	60 seconds	30 seconds on each leg
	Plank	30–60 seconds	Builds endurance in abdominal muscles and back
	Double-leg jump	60 seconds	Land as softly as possible
	Side plank	60 seconds	Strengthens oblique abdominal muscles
	Upright row	30 seconds	Use water bottles as weights
	Side crunch	60 seconds	30 seconds on each side
	Bicep curl	30 seconds	Use water bottles as weights
Three	Walking, marching on spot	5 minutes L1–L2	Warm up
	Wide-leg power squat	60 seconds	Exercises quadriceps
	Decline press-up	30 seconds	Build up to 60 seconds; put feet on chair or bed
	Leg criss-cross	30 seconds	Build up to 60 seconds
	Superman	60 seconds	Works buttocks and abdominal muscles
	Lateral jump	60 seconds	Strengthens and tones the thighs, hamstrings and buttocks
	Lateral raise	30 seconds	Use water bottles as weights
	Reverse crunch	60 seconds	Works lower abdominal muscles
	Triceps press-up	30 seconds	Build up to 60 seconds
	Single-leg hip raise	60 seconds	30 seconds on each leg

Above and left: You don't have to give up exercising if you are travelling; you can manage without any equipment.

Speed and Power Plan

Training for speed and power calls for a very fine balancing act. You need to get faster and stronger, but without adding too much muscle bulk, which will only slow you down. This plan will help you to fine-tune your training strategy.

Plyometrics and sprint training will help train your fast-twitch muscle fibres to give you the increased speed and power you want. However, without initial resistance training to develop strong muscles, you may find it difficult to increase your speed and power.

Follow this plan for six weeks, using the One Repetition Maximum (ORM) test for strength and timed sprints to see if you are getting faster. The speed and power training plan gives you the structure of the programme for a week.

Exercise exchange
After three weeks, you can try exchanging some of the exercises with other, similar, exercises. For example introduce some other resistance training exercises for legs to challenge your muscles in different ways. You could change hack squats for leg presses, and the single-leg hip raise with cable

> **Layered clothing**
> It is important to keep your muscles warm throughout your training session, especially when you want them to perform powerfully with fast contractions. The solution is to wear a number of layers of clothing, so that you can easily adjust them to suit your level of intensity and the conditions in which you are training.

kick backs. Do the same for your upper-body exercises. Adjusting the exercises and changing the order will challenge your body further, making it faster and stronger. Include some core-stability training every week. Your core muscles will play a vital role in helping you to avoid injury and enable you to create forward speed, with all your muscles recruiting in the correct order.

Above: To gain speed and power, you may consider taking extra protein in the form of drinks, which you can make from a protein powder formula.

Speed and power training plan
Always do 5 to 10 minutes' cardiovascular warm-up, which should be at a higher intensity than a warm-up for normal gym training. You need to get as much blood as possible circulating to the big muscles that you want to use. Follow the warm-up with stretches, to prepare your body for the hard training session. Stretch your muscles at the end of the workout to help them recover and avoid injury. Your speed and power should be much improved if you stick to this plan for about six weeks.

Day	Exercise	Time/Sets/Reps/Level	Comments
Monday	Running	10 minutes L1–L2	Warm up
	8 x 100m/109-yd sprints	L4	Stretch to prevent injury
	300m/328-yd jog recovery	L1	Stretch to help recovery
	8 x 50m sprints	L4	Don't overstride, keep to 90 strides per minute
	350m/383-yd jog recovery	L1	Try to maintain good technique
	Running	5 minutes L1	Cool down
Tuesday	Cycling	5 minutes L1–L2	Warm up
	Hack squat	5 x 8–10	Exercises quadriceps muscles
	Dead lift	5 x 8–10	Works thighs and buttocks
	Wide-leg power squat	5 x 8–10	Works the quadriceps muscles
	Dumbbell squat	5 x 8–10	Tones buttocks, hips and thighs
	Lunge	5 x 8–10	Try bench drop lunges to make it harder
	Calf raise	5 x 8–10	Use weights to make it harder
	Single-leg hip raise	3 x 20	Tones and strengthens the buttocks

Day	Exercise	Time/Sets/Reps/Level	Comments
Wednesday	Cycling	5 minutes L1–L2	Warm up
	Double-leg squat jump	5 x 20	To prevent injury, make sure your plyometrics technique is correct
	Side lateral jumps	5 x 20	Works quadriceps and buttocks
	Single-leg squat jump	5 x 20	10 each leg
	Step-up	5 x 20	10 each leg
	Crunch	3 x 20	Workout for the abdominals
	Hanging leg raises	3 x 20	Begin with 10, build up to 20
	Knee cable rotations	3 x 20	Exercises abdominal muscles
Thursday	Running	10 minutes L1–L2	Warm up
	4 x 200m/219-yd sprint	L4	Develops fast-twitch muscle fibres
	200m/219-yd jog recovery	L1	Use good technique for stretching, don't bounce
	6 x 100m/109-yd sprint	L4	Helps increase speed and power
	200m/219-yd jog recovery	L1	Aids easy recovery between sprint efforts
	8 x 50m/55-yd sprint	L4	Increases leg turnover
	150m/164-yd jog recovery	L1	Stretching actually encourages relaxation
	Running	5 minutes L1	Cool down
Friday	Running	40 minutes L2–L4	Use the first 5–10 minutes to warm up to L1, then 10–20-second sprints at L4 every 3 minutes
Saturday	Rowing	5 minutes L1–L2	Warm up
	Overhand chin-up, wide grip	5 x max reps	Develops back muscles
	Olympic bar chest press	5 x 8–10	Tones and shapes the chest
	Bent-over barbell row	5 x 8–10	Strengthens the back muscles
	Dumbbell chest press, incline bench	5 x 8–10	Builds up the chest, shoulder and arms
	Arnie shoulder press	5 x 8–10	Srengthens shoulders and upper arms
	Cable frontal raise	5 x 8–10	Works front of shoulders
	Dumbbell bicep curls	5 x 8–10	Optimum workout for the biceps
	Triceps cable push-down	5 x 8–10	Works the triceps
	Bench triceps dip	3 x max reps	Strengthens triceps
Sunday	Rest day	24 hours	Eases and repairs sore muscles

Nutrition

You can increase the density of your muscles by stepping up the calorie content of your diet. Study the information on how you should eat to gain muscle. Always have a recovery drink, consisting of a mixture of carbohydrate and protein, to aid a speedy recovery and prepare your muscles for their next training session, or recovery between sessions could be twice as long.

Right: Gaining speed and power won't just happen overnight; it will take time, hard work and dedication to your training plan.

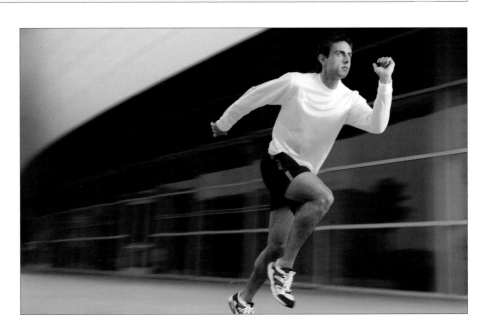

Racket Sports Plan

Playing racket sports – particularly tennis, squash and badminton – is a good and highly enjoyable way of keeping fit and competing with a partner. It can also be one of the best ways to de-stress after a hard day's work.

Racket sports demand a great deal of your time if you are to play them properly and enjoy them to the full, with a competitive edge: you need power, speed, stamina and good stability.

Boost your fitness
With such intense physical demands, you need to do more for your fitness than just play the game – no matter how regularly you practice. Take time to complete these two sessions in every ten-day period to give you the best chance of improving your game and preventing injury. You will soon find that you can get to the ball quicker and make it harder for your opponent to get a winning shot past you.

It is vital that you do regular core-stability training at least once a week to prepare your body for the constant pounding and change of direction. Begin with basic core exercises and work your way up to the advanced exercises and the fit ball, BOSU and medicine ball exercises.

On the days between racket and gym sessions, you should focus on building up your cardiovascular fitness with a

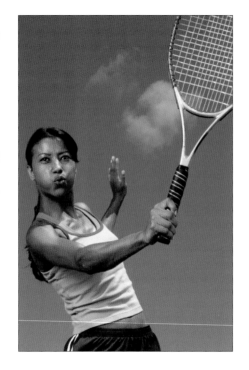

Above: Reaching a good standard in racket sports takes a lot of effort. It also requires strength and stamina so that you can last out in a long game.

Below: Core-stability exercises are essential to avoid injuries and they will help to make you a better player.

Above: Fluid intake will have a beneficial effect on your performance. If you are dehydrated, you lack concentration and feel under par.

Below: Rotational exercises will help your reflexes become sharper and will make you a good competitor.

Racket sports exercise plan

Before you play any competitive racket sport or start a training session, always try to fit in at least 5 to 10 minutes' warm-up, consisting of activities such as walking and jogging, cycling or rowing, followed by a warm-down of some stretches. Also, it is a good idea to stretch after your tennis game or training session to help your muscles to recover faster and avoid injury.

Session	Exercise	Time/Sets/Reps/Level	Comments
One	Cycling	5–20 minutes L1–L2	Warm up; option to row or run
	Leg press	3 x 20	Firms and tones leg muscles
	Side lunge	3 x 20	Strengthens hips, buttocks and thighs
	Step-up	3 x 20	Tones and firms leg muscles
	Rowing	10–20 minutes	2 minutes at L2 and 1 minute at L4
	Lateral pull-down, overarm grip	3 x 12–15	Works the lats (muscles in the back)
	Dumbbell chest press, incline bench	3 x 12–15	Builds up the chest, shoulders, arms
	Arnie shoulder press	3 x 12–15	Strengthens shoulders and upper arms
	Crunch	3 x 20	Abdominal workout
	Reverse crunch	3 x 20	Tones and strengthens rectus abdominis
	Oblique crunch	3 x 20	Works upper abdominals and obliques
	Dumbbell bicep curl	3 x 12	Optimum workout for the biceps
	Bench triceps dip	3 x 20	Exercises triceps
Two	Rowing	5 minutes L1–L2	Warm up; option to use bike
	Plank	30–60 seconds	Builds up abdominals and back
	Superman	3 x10	Works buttocks and abdominal muscles
	Hip raise	3 x 20	Tones and strengthens the buttocks
	Press-up to dumbbell row	3 x 20	Good for core stability
	Double-leg jump	3 x 20	Builds power and speed
	Lateral jump	3 x 20	Strengthens the thighs, hamstrings and buttocks
	Overhead slam	3 x 10	Engages buttocks, chest and abdominals
	Single-leg squat with cable row to frontal raise, start position	3 x 10	Reinforces a strong core
	Cable wood chop, high to low	3 x 10	10 each side
	Dumbbell side bend	3 x 20	Works obliques and abdominal muscles

20- to 40-minute run. Also, make sure to vary the pace of the run to simulate the varying pace in the rackets game. Include five to ten 20-second sprints and some 30–60-second hill intervals.

Nutrition

Racket sports combine many attributes of fitness, making them a great way to lose weight. However, it is always important to eat healthily and include a mixture of low and medium GI foods that contain adequate protein to help your muscles recover and strengthen.

As with all intense physical activity, you need to be careful not to become dehydrated during the game. Always have a water bottle nearby and use energy drinks to keep hydrated if you know you will be playing or training for more than an hour.

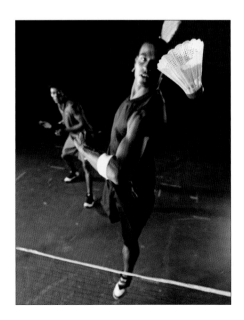

Below: In racket sports, there is demand on the muscles to contract fast so that you can leap into the air.

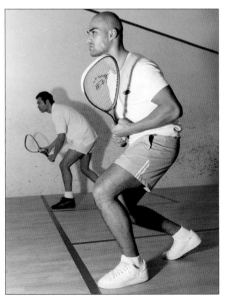

Below: Fitness will enable you to get into position faster to return the opposition's shot.

Golf Plan

It may look like an amiable, leisurely pastime, but golf is a very complex sport that involves high-speed muscular movements with rotation and which, at the same time, demands a solid base as well as great focus and control.

To become a better golfer, you have to practise as much as possible – there are no short cuts. As with many other sports, however, it is not just a matter of practising the game itself. In fact, in order to be able to practise for long periods of time using such a complex muscular movement, you will have to be fit. Otherwise, your body will simply

Below: One of the main goals when training for golf is to remain free from any injury by building up fitness.

break down through overuse injuries, which will prevent you from improving, or even enjoying, your game.

The two sessions outlined here will help you work the muscles you need for the golf swing, which will, in turn, help to improve your game and avoid injury. Session one aims to build basic strength to enable your muscles to train harder for longer. Session two is more advanced: it uses rotational exercises with balance and core stability to simulate the stresses on the body during

Above: A long round of golf will make you dehydrated, especially in hot weather, so always carry a drink with you when you are on the course.

your golf swing. It is important to use one side of the body at a time for some of your resistance exercises, as golf will affect your muscular symmetry. To prevent injury, the muscles on both sides of your body need to be well balanced.

The key to great golf

Flexibility and core stability are essential attributes for a successful golfer. Core stability, in fact, is perhaps more important for golf than for any other sport. One slight wrong movement in your trunk could have a detrimental effect on your golf swing. Make sure you progress through the core-stability exercises, beginning at the basic level.

Flexibility is also a major factor in golf; you need to be able to rotate at the trunk with great flexibility, so take time to

Switch on core muscles

Try to fit in some basic core exercises just before you tee off. They will help you to switch on the core muscles so that they support your game from the first stroke onward.

Golf exercise plan

On days between your twice-weekly gym sessions, you should try to improve your cardiovascular fitness to improve your aerobic efficiency and stamina on the golf course. Do 20–40 minutes of some form of cardiovascular exercise, such as running, rowing, cycling or cross-training twice a week. The fitter you are, the more energy you will have to focus on your game.

Session	Exercise	Time/Sets/Reps/Level	Comments
One	Rowing	5–10 minutes L1–L2	Warm up; option of cycling or cross-trainer
	Dumbbell squat	3 x 20	Progress to single-leg squats
	Side lunge	3 x 20	10 to each side
	Single-leg squat	3 x 20	10 on each leg. Focus on keeping your hips level
	Single-arm cable lat pull-down	3 x 12–15	On each arm
	Bent-over barbell row	3 x 12–15	Strengthens the back
	Cable fly, standing	3 x 12–15	Develops pectorals
	Arnie shoulder press	3 x 12–15	Strengthens shoulders and upper arms
	Bent-over lateral raise	3 x 12–15	Exercises shoulders and back
	Single-arm triceps cable push-down	3 x 12–15	Mainly works the triceps
	Wrist curl	3 x 12–15	Change the angle of the wrist curl every session
	Oblique crunches	3 x 20	10 each side
Two	Rowing	5–10 minutes L1–L2	Warm up; option of cycling or cross-trainer
	BOSU squat	3 x 20	Progress to single-leg BOSU squat
	Plank knee tuck	3 x 20	10 each side
	Cable wood chop on BOSU	3 x 20	Begin without BOSU, progressing to standing BOSU
	Single-hand medicine ball press-up	3 x 20	10 each arm
	Medicine ball lunge and lean	3 x 20	10 each leg
	Medicine ball lunge and rotate	3 x 20	10 each leg
	Squat to cable shoulder press	3 x 20	Begin with 10 reps and build up to 20
	Press-up to dumbbell row	3 x 20	10 rows each arm
	Squat to cable side twist	3 x 20	20 each side
	High cable side bend	3 x 20	Movement works the abdominals

do regular stretching before and after every practice session and game. If your muscles are not flexible, you will become increasingly prone to injury, and you will not be able to get your body into the positions necessary for a great golf swing.

Nutrition

The longer your golf game, the more important your nutrition. If you play 18 holes, you will typically walk 8–10km/ 5–6 miles, perhaps also carrying your clubs. Eat the correct foods before, during and after the game, and stay well hydrated. Eat low GI foods for a slow, steady release of energy. Always have a drink with you to prevent dehydration, especially during the hot summer months.

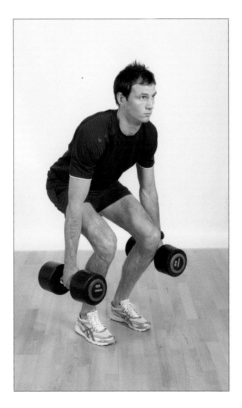

Right: Squats are a great way to build up strength in the leg muscles, and increase your fitness for golf.

Above: Side stretches will help you to stay flexible, which is essential for golf.

Contact Sports Plan

Contact sports rely on many different fitness attributes. Which one you choose, and how you tailor your fitness plan, depends on whether you want to focus on your speed, power, strength, endurance, stability or flexibility.

Contact sports range from team sports, such as rugby and football, to individual sports, such as boxing and martial arts like tae kwon do. For a team contact sport, such as rugby, you should train according to the position you play in. For example, if you are a forward, you will want to be strong and powerful, so you should concentrate on heavy resistance training with low repetitions and increased emphasis on your upper body. If you play in the back rows, you will need speed and stability to be able to run fast and

Below: In contact sports, stability is vital if you are to avoid being injured. You also need flexibility and speed.

change direction. You will also need some muscular strength to take the tackles and take on the opposition, so your training plan should include a mixture of resistance-training and core-stability exercises, with particular emphasis on plyometrics.

Train and adapt

The three sessions outlined here will give you a basic fitness level that you can then progress from and adapt. Between your three weekly gym sessions, do regular cardiovascular training. Most of this can be undertaken during actual practice in your sport, but extra cardiovascular training will give you an added advantage.

Above: If you have access to a gym before your sport, you can warm up using the cross-trainer.

Try to do two 40-minute runs, mixed with ten hill sprints of 10–20 seconds and ten flat sprints lasting 10–20 seconds, to get your body used to high-intensity workouts and faster recovery. A weekly boxercise session will prepare you for hand–eye co-ordination and improve cardiovascular fitness and upper-body strength.

Core stability and flexibility

To help prevent injury and enable you to use all your strength, speed and power effectively, core stability is vital. Work your way through basic, intermediate and advanced core-stability training sessions for the best results. Flexibility in contact sports is often neglected, so make time to stretch once you are warmed up, and exercise to let your muscles prepare for training and fast recovery.

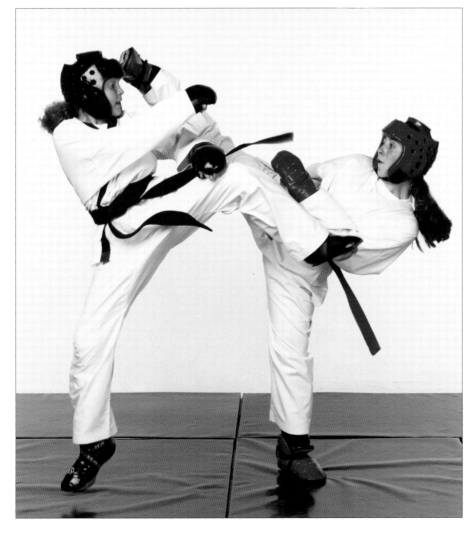

Contact sports exercise plan

Session one works your legs, session two works your upper body and session three is partly for speed and partly for trunk stability. If your sport requires more endurance and less muscle bulk, increase to 12–15 repetitions for each set during the resistance exercises.

Session	Exercise	Time/Sets/Reps/Level	Comments
One	Rowing	5–10 minutes L1–L2	Warm up; option to cycle, run or use cross-trainer
	Hack squat	5 x 8–10	Good for upper legs and buttocks
	Dead lift	5 x 8–10	Works thighs and buttocks
	Single-leg squat	5 x 8–10	With dumbbells
	Step-up	5 x 8–10	With dumbbells
	Lunge	5 x 8–10	On each leg, holding dumbbells
	Cable adductor/abductor	5 x 8—10	Works strong muscles in upper legs
	Calf raise	5 x 8–10	Use weights to make it harder
	Crunch	3 x 20	Hold weights in hands above head to make it harder
	Reverse crunch	3 x 20	Abdominal workout
	Hanging leg raise with twist	3 x 10	Build up to 20 reps
Two	Rowing	5–10 minutes L1–L2	Warm up; option to cycle, run or use cross-trainer
	Over-arm chin-up, wide grip	5 x max reps	Exercises the lats, biceps and mid back
	Dumbbell chest press, flat bench	5 x 8–10	Develops and tones the chest
	Single-arm dumbbell row	5 x 8–10	Workout for the middle back muscles
	Press-up	5 x 8–10	Strengthens back, chest and arms
	Cable shoulder press	5 x 8–10	Strengthens upper arms, improves general fitness
	Arnie shoulder press	5 x 8–10	Strengthens shoulders and upper arms
	Bent-over cable lateral raise	5 x 8–10	Develops rear deltoid (shoulder) muscles
	Sit-up with Russian twist	3 x 20	Works abdominals and obliques
	Oblique crunch	3 x 20	Works upper abdominals and obliques
	Dumbbell side bends	3 x 20	Works obliques and abdominal muscles
Three	Row	5–10 minutes L1–L2	Warm up; option to cycle, run or use cross-trainer
	Double-leg jump	3 x 20	Good core stability needed for this jump
	Lateral jump	3 x 20	Strengthens and tones the thighs, hamstrings and buttocks
	Lunge jump	3 x 20	Good for buttocks, quadriceps and calf muscles
	Squat throw	3 x 20	Strengthens core muscles of abdomen, hip and buttocks
	Over head slam	3 x 20	Engages hamstrings, hips and buttocks
	Press-up to dumbbell row	3 x 20	Good exercise for core stability
	Dumbbell bicep curl	3 x 8–10	Optimum workout for the biceps
	Bench triceps dip	3 x max reps	Keep legs straight to make it harder
	Broomstick twist	3 x 20	Works obliques: the muscles at the side of abdomen
	Kneeling cable rotation	3 x 20	Exercises the abdominals
	Side crunches	3 x 20	Strengthens and tones obliques
	Warm down	5–10 minutes	Stretches

Nutrition

You will need to adjust your nutrition depending on what it is you want to achieve. In order to lose weight, to gain muscle, or to increase your endurance choose a diet that is appropriate for your requirements.

Right: Resistance training will help your body take the physical knocks from the opposition without injury.

Swimming Plan

There is more to becoming a good swimmer than just being able to dive in and swim a few lengths in the pool. The training plan outlined here will improve your fitness level in the water and give you greater strength.

Choose two of the three training sessions outlined here to do on the days you are not swimming at high intensity. If you are going to do resistance training on the same day as swim training, then decide which session you want to get the most out of and do that first. Be aware that the resistance training may leave you feeling sluggish in the water later in the day. However, if you swim first, you may struggle to make the improvements you want in your resistance training.

Core stability and flexibility

To form a strong connection between your upper and lower body, you need to have strong core stability. There is no point in having strong shoulders and legs if the centre of your body is weak, as this will only result in energy loss when training or competing. So, begin with the basic core-stability exercises,

Below: Regular stretching of the arms will keep your muscles long and powerful for swimming.

Above: Stretch your body after swimming, paying particular attention to the arms and shoulders.

twice a week, gradually building up at your own pace to the intermediate and advanced exercises.

In order to get a full range of movement for all swim strokes, it is important to stay flexible, so regularly stretch all areas of your body after every session in the pool or the gym.

Above: Stretch your neck to avoid it getting stiff from trying to lift your head, or turn the neck to the side to breathe.

In particular you should pay careful attention to your back, chest, shoulders and arms.

Nutrition

Consume low to medium GI foods every three to four hours and eat high GI foods during training sessions.

Stay well hydrated when you are swimming. It's easy to think you don't need anything to drink because you are exercising in water – however, some pools can be hot, which can dehydrate you. Always have a water bottle at the side of the pool.

Right: Always have the right equipment, such as goggles, so that you can relax and enjoy your swim.

Swimming exercise plan

All three of these sessions include a combination of upper- and lower-body exercises as well as exercises to build abdominal strength. If you have weak areas, you can spend more time on them. For example, if you have weak shoulders, you may want to include more shoulder exercises.

Session	Exercise	Time/Sets/Reps/Level	Comments
One	Row	5–10 minutes L1–L2	Warm up; option to use cross-trainer
	Overhand chin-up, wide grip	3 x max reps	Develops shoulders and upper back
	Olympic bar chest press	3 x 10–12	Tones and shapes the chest
	Overhand lateral pull-down, wide grip	3 x 10–12	Targets the lats
	Cable fly	3 x 10–12	Develops pectorals
	Leg press	3 x 20	Strengthens and firms leg muscles
	Leg extension	3 x 20	Strengthens and works upper legs
	Arnie shoulder press	3 x 10–12	Strengthens shoulders and upper arms
	Cable triceps push-down	3 x 10–12	Exercises triceps
	Reverse crunch	3 x 20	Tones and strengthens rectus abdominis
	Hanging leg raise	3 x 20	Builds up the abdominal muscles
Two	Cross-trainer	5–10 minutes L1–L2	Warm up; option to use rowing machine
	Seated cable row	3 x 10–12	Strengthens the middle back and forearms
	Dumbbell chest press, incline bench	3 x 10–12	Builds up the chest, shoulder and arms
	Single-arm cable lateral pull-down	3 x 10–12	Each arm
	Medicine ball one-hand press-up	3 x 10–12	Each arm
	Hack squat	3 x 20	Good for upper legs and buttocks
	Machine leg curl	3 x 20	Exercises the hamstrings
	Dumbbell frontal raise	3 x 10–12	Each arm
	Overhead triceps extension	3 x 10–12	Increases strength and flexibility of the triceps
	Oblique crunch	3 x 20	Works upper abdominals and obliques
	Broomstick twist	3 x 20	Works obliques: the muscles at side of abdomen
Three	Rowing	5–10 minutes L1–L2	Warm up; option to use cross-trainer
	Single-arm dumbbell row	3 x 10–12	Workout for the middle back muscles
	Dumbbell chest press, decline bench	3 x 10–12	Targets the pectoral muscles
	Single-arm straight arm pull-down	3 x 10–12	Exercise aimed at outer back
	Dumbbell fly, flat bench	3 x 10–12	Strengthens chest
	Lunge	3 x 20	10 on each leg
	Calf raise	3 x 20	Strengthens the calf muscles
	Cable lateral raise	3 x 10–12	Each arm
	Single-leg squat to cable row to frontal raise	3 x 10–12	Each arm
	Dumbbell biceps curl	3 x 10–12	Develops biceps
	Kneeling cable rotation	3 x 20	10 each side
	Cable side bend	3 x 20	Works the oblique muscles of the abdomen

Running Plan

Being a successful runner involves more than simply running. You need to do the correct core-stability and resistance-exercise training for support and to help you to avoid injuries. You also need gradually to increase the distances that you run.

The distance of your running event, for example, a marathon or a 5km/3-mile race, will dictate the amount of running that you have to do. You should aim to run three to four times a week, varying the distances, speeds, inclines and length of intervals to challenge your body and improve your fitness. Do not run more than two days in a row unless you are an elite runner, as this will make you prone to injury. If you want to do cardiovascular training on other days, choose low-impact exercises, such as cycling, rowing or swimming.

The cross-trainer is an excellent tool for keeping fit if you are recovering from a running injury, because it works the running muscles using similar movement patterns to running.

Below: To improve running times, use exercises that are directly related to the same movements.

Core-stability and resistance training

Your fitness training programme should involve resistance training twice weekly and regular core-stability training. Begin with basic level core-stability training, then gradually work your way up to the intermediate and advanced exercises. Core stability is essential for running because of the constant impact on one leg and the resulting lateral movement, which can cause injury. Do some core-stability exercises immediately before your fastest runs so that your core muscles are already switched on before you start running.

Resistance training will give you the strength to resist the constant impact of running and provide the power to drive you forward, thus making you faster. Do the resistance-training exercises on the days that you are not running. Do not, however, do a resistance session before going for a run, as your muscles will be tired and therefore unable to support you adequately while you run. This is only likely to make you more prone to injury.

Above: Run with people of your own ability to avoid injury, and push yourself to make improvements.

Stretching

It is important to stretch before and after every session. The main muscles that you need to pay attention to are the lower back, hamstrings, quadriceps, hip flexors and calf muscles. Take 5 minutes to complete your stretches – they are just as important as running or resistance training.

Nutrition

Being lightweight is an advantage for runners, so eat healthily to keep your weight low, choosing foods that are low to medium GI, and eat regularly to keep your metabolism high and help your body to recover between training sessions. In the 2 hours before, as well as during and immediately after a long running session, eat a mixture of low and high GI foods to enable faster recovery and to replace muscle glycogen (stored glucose).

Exercise plan for runners

Session one and two will strengthen your running muscles. Session three works some of the smaller muscles and helps combine the core and major muscles used in running. Session four is for the upper body. You should do all of these exercises at least once every two weeks to maintain upper-body strength and muscle tone.

Session	Exercise	Time/Sets/Reps/Level	Comments
One	Running	5–10 minutes L1–L2	Warm up
	Leg press	3 x 20	Strengthens and firms leg muscles
	Dumbbell squat	3 x 20	Tones buttocks, hips and thighs
	Crunch	3 x 20	Abominal workout
	Step-up	3 x 20	Exercises and tones leg muscles
	Lunge	3 x 20	Works the upper leg and buttocks
	Reverse crunch	3 x 20	Tones and strengthens rectus abdominis
	Leg extension	3 x 20	Strengthens and works upper legs
	Calf raise	3 x 20+	Strengthens the calf muscles
	Oblique crunch	3 x 20	Works upper abdominals and obliques
	Dumbbell side bend	3 x 20	Works obliques and abdominal muscles
Two	Running	5–10 minutes L1–L2	Warm up
	Hack squat	3 x 20	Good for upper legs and buttocks
	Dead lift	3 x 20	Works thighs and buttocks
	Leg criss-cross	3 x 20	Tones the abdominal muscles
	Side step-up	3 x 20	Works leg muscles
	Side lunge	3 x 20	Strengthens hips, buttocks and thighs
	Broomstick twist	3 x 20	Works the muscles at the side of the abdomen
	Leg curl	3 x 20	Exercises the hamstrings
	Calf raise	3 x 20+	Strengthens the calf muscles
	Kneeling cable rotation	3 x 20	Exercises the abdominals
	High cable side bend	3 x 20	Movement works the abdominals
	Dumbbell bicep curl	3 x 20	Optimum workout for the biceps
Three	Run	5–10 minutes L1–L2	Warm up
	Cable hip adduction	3 x 20	Improves stability
	Cable hip abduction	3 x 20	Targets hip abductor muscles and buttocks
	Cable kick back	3 x 20	Strengthens buttocks and hamstrings
	V-crunch	3 x 20	Works 'six-pack' abdominal muscles
	BOSU squat	3 x 20	Progress to single-leg squats
	Gluteal bridge	3 x 20	Progress to feet on fit ball
	Medicine ball, lunge and lean	3 x 20	Builds strength and power
	Medicine ball, lunge and rotate	3 x 20	Improves link between upper, lower and core muscles
	Press-up to dumbbell rows	3 x 20	Good exercise for core stability
	Sit-up with Russian twist	3 x 20	Works abdominals and obliques
Four	Run	5–10 minutes L1–L2	Warm up
	Lateral pull-down	3 x 12–15	Works the lats (muscles in the back)
	Dumbbell chest press	3 x 12–15	Workout of the upper arm, chest and shoulder
	Seated cable row	3 x 12–15	Strengthens the middle back and forearms
	Cable fly	3 x 12–15	Develops pectorals
	Arnie shoulder press	3 x 12–15	Strengthens shoulders and upper arms
	Bent-over dumbbell lateral raise	3 x 12–15	Strengthens upper back and shoulders
	Dumbbell frontal raise	3 x 12–15	Exercises shoulders
	Bench triceps dip	3 x 12–15	Exercises triceps
	Cable bicep curls	3 x 12–15	Develops and strengthens biceps
	Warm down	5–10 minutes	Leg stretches

Cycling Plan

Cycling may appear to be an easy way to get fit and, up to a point, it is. Taking it one step farther, however, by increasing your strength and power to enable you to cycle faster, for longer, calls for a detailed plan.

There are many different types of cycling disciplines, including track racing, long-distance stage races, cross-country, mountain biking, downhill mountain biking and cyclo-cross, to name but a few. They all require slightly different types of training intensity and duration.

The information on page 48 tells you how to set up your bike correctly and the type of session that you can include in your training to make you go faster. However, as with many of the sports covered in this book, if you want to become really good at cycling, you need to get off your bike and into the gym.

Core-stability and resistance training

You will need to undertake core-stability training twice a week to strengthen your trunk muscles and help support your back, especially the lower

Above: Track cycling requires huge amounts of training and power to win races.

Below: Cycling off-road requires considerable effort and hence demands a lot of your core-stability muscles.

back, if you are to become a more proficient cyclist. The bent-forward position of the cyclist requires you to have a strong core, as a weak core will soon result in an aching back. Core-stability training will also make your muscles recruit in the correct order and help you to avoid lateral movement, thus ensuring that all your power is going into driving the bike forward, rather than being lost sideways, especially when you are climbing hills out of the saddle. So, begin with the basic core exercises and gradually build up to the intermediate and advanced exercises.

Resistance training will help you to become more powerful. Remember that the stronger the engine, the greater the potential for speed. You should do two resistance-training sessions per week, focusing on your legs, along with a small number of upper-body exercises. It is also vital that you stay flexible, so always remember to do some stretching after every cycle ride or fitness training session in the gym.

Below: Having the fitness and strong legs able to shift your body weight is essential for cycling. This lunge will help to build up the leg muscles.

Nutrition

For obvious reasons, lightweight cyclists are better cyclists. The heavier you are, the more weight you have to move, especially when it comes to going uphill. You should, therefore, eat a diet consisting mainly of low to medium GI foods to keep your weight down and maintain your energy levels. Eating every three to four hours will help to maintain a high metabolism and allow your muscles to recover faster between training sessions. In the two hours before, as well as during and after long rides, eat a mixture of low and high GI foods to aid faster recovery and to replace muscle glycogen (glucose stored in the muscles).

Right: When you are cycling in remote areas, eat low and high GI foods regularly to maintain the metabolism.

Exercise plan for cyclists

Session one and two will provide basic muscular strength. Session three is more advanced and involves working your core muscles and limbs at the same time. Try to do each of these three sessions within a period of ten days.

Session	Exercise	Time/Sets/Reps/Level	Comments
One	Cycling	5–10 minutes L1–L2	Warm up
	Hack squat	3 x 20	Good for upper legs and buttocks
	Dead lift	3 x 20	Works thighs and buttocks
	Leg extension	3 x 20	Try doing this with just one leg
	Lunge	3 x 20	10 each leg; hold dumbbells to make it harder
	Side lunge	3 x 20	10 to each side
	Cable adductor	3 x 20	10 each leg
	Cable kickback	3 x 20	10 each leg
	Crunch	3 x 20	Workout for the abdominals
	Oblique crunch	3 x 20	Works upper abdominals and obliques
	Arnie shoulder press	3 x 12–15	Strengthens shoulders and upper arms
	Dumbbell biceps curl	3 x 12–15	Develops biceps
Two	Cycling	5–10 minutes L1–L2	Warm up
	Leg press	3 x 20	Try using single legs
	Dumbbell squats	3 x 20	Progress to one-leg squats
	Leg curl	3 x 20	Try using single legs
	Step-up	3 x 20	10 each leg; hold dumbbells to make it harder
	Side step-up	3 x 20	10 each leg
	Cable abductor	3 x 20	10 each leg
	Calf raise	3 x 20+	Strengthens the calf muscles
	Reverse crunch	3 x 20	Tones and strengthens rectus abdominis
	Side crunch	3 x 2	Strengthens and tones obliques
	Cable lateral raise	3 x 12–15	Develops shoulder muscles
	Triceps cable push-down	3 x 12–15	Strengthens triceps muscles
Three	Cycling	5–10 minutes L1–L2	Warm-up
	Medicine ball lunges with leans	3 x 20	10 each side
	Medicine ball, lunges with rotations	3 x 20	10 each side
	Squat to cable shoulder press	3 x 20	Exercises the legs and shoulders
	Press-up to dumbbell row	3 x 10	Good exercise for core stability
	Squat throw	3 x 10	Strengthens core muscles of abdomen, hip and buttocks
	Single-leg squat with cable row to frontal raise	3 x 20	10 each side – good for developing balance and stability
	Lunge with medicine ball to wood chop	3 x 20	10 each side
	Kneeling cable rotations	3 x 20	10 each side

Triathlon Training Plan

With their intense determination and high pain threshold, triathletes are prone to overuse injuries. A sensible training plan, including strength and core-stability training, can reduce these risks and help them achieve their full potential.

Triathlon is one of the fastest growing sports in the world. Triathlon is usually taken seriously and training is to prepare for the competition. Perhaps one of the reasons it is so popular is because many competitors are good or were good at one or two of the disciplines, and having reached the peak in one of those, they want a new challenge. Competition is more attractive than in other endurance sports since you can race against people of similar age and ability as well as being on the course with the world's best.

Base training

Aim to do three key training sessions – one swim, one cycle, one run – each week to see a progressive improvement.

These sessions require your full focus and energy to get the most out of them. The other three sessions in the week are base sessions that provide increased aerobic and strength maintenance, which will enable your three key sessions to be more beneficial. Without these base sessions you will be prone to over-training and injuries. The key sessions should be two days apart and adapted to the distances you do in competition. For example, if you are training for an Ironman competition, you will need to do one swim of between 65 and 90 minutes, one cycle ride lasting up to 6 hours, and one run lasting between 80 and 120 minutes. If you want to compete in Olympic distance triathlons

you will need to do one swim lasting between 20 and 40 minutes, one cycle ride lasting over 90 minutes and one run lasting between 40 and 60 minutes.

Transition

The transition (movement from one form of exercise to another) in triathlon from swim to bike and bike to run is one of the most difficult parts of this sport. When you leave the water after the swimming it is hard to get your legs working as efficiently as you would want them to because all the oxygenated blood has been sent to your upper body to help in the swim. It can take a few minutes before you really feel your legs working. To help make this transition

---

Strength and core-training exercises

These exercise sessions should form part of your training plan, twice a week, right up to the week of the actual race itself.

Session	Exercise	Time/Sets/Reps/Level	Comments
One	Rowing	5–10 minutes L1–L2	Warm up
	Lat pull-down, wide grip	3 x 12	Exercises the muscles of the back
	Single-arm cable pull-down	3 x 12	Works lats, also biceps and middle back
	Press-up to single-arm dumbbell row	3 x 12	Begin with 5 on each arm and build up to 12
	Plank	3 x 60 seconds	Begin with 10 seconds and build up to 60
	Medicine ball press-up	3 x 12	Begin with 5 on each arm and build up to 12
	Medicine ball throw-down	3 x 20	Builds strength and stability
	Dumbbell lat raise	3 x 12	Exercises the shoulders
	Dumbbell frontal raise	3 x 12	Exercises the shoulders
	Bench triceps dip	3 x 20	Exercises triceps
	Hanging leg raise	3 x 10	Builds up the abdominal muscles
	Crunch with Russian twist	3 x 20	Strengthens the abdominals and lower back
Two	Cycling	5–10 minutes L1–L2	Warm up
	Lunges with twists	3 x 20	10 each side
	Lunges with medicine ball wood chops	3 x 20	10 each side
	Fit ball sit-up	3 x 20	Exercises the abdominal muscles
	Machine leg curl	3 x 20	Try using single legs
	Single-leg squat	3 x 10	Works gluteus, hamstrings, quadriceps and core muscles
	Side plank	3 x 60-second holds	Begin with 10 seconds and build up to 60
	Single-leg hip raise	3 x 10	Workout for the buttocks
	Calf raises	3 x 20	Strengthens the calf muscles
	Side crunch	3 x 20	Strengthens and tones obliques

Above: During the swim part of the triathlon, keep focused and try to ignore the other competitors.

smoother in competition try and practise the transition from swim to bike as frequently as you can so that you can quickly adapt from one sport to another. As you leave the swim try and kick more with your legs to distribute more blood to your legs and prepare them for running out of the water and on to the bike section. For the transition of bike to run you have to tackle the problem of trying to stride out. Your stride length on the bike is very short as it is just the length of the cranks, which can lead to tightening of the muscles in the hips and back of legs, mainly the hamstrings and calf muscles.

This is a common time for injuries to occur. To prevent this from happening use a short stride pattern for the first few minutes of the run and then gently lengthen your stride allowing your muscles to stretch out and give you an effective stride length. Practise your transition from bike to run in training but be careful about when you do your bike-to-run transitions. In training, avoid

bike-to-run sessions after long hard bike sessions. The long bike ride will make the muscles in your legs tired. Not only do your leg muscles need to be fresh to power you forward on the run, they also need to act as shock absorbers to absorb the impact as your feet strike the ground. Tired legs going into the run may make you more prone to injuries, so make sure you engage your core muscles when your legs feel tired to support your body properly. Speed of transition is important as your time in

Above: Lat pull-downs work the muscles in the back. A strong back is essential when competing in a triathlon.

transition is included in your overall time. You need the appropriate equipment to make transitions faster and to practise changing out of swim gear into bike gear and going from bike

Below: Transition from swim to run can make your legs feel weak, so practise it many times beforehand.

Above: The longer the distance of the triathlon, the more influential the bike leg will be on the overall result.

gear to running gear. Saving a few minutes in transition is easier than trying to make up 2 minutes on the bike or run.

Equipment

Choosing the correct equipment is vital if you are to feel at ease during every stage of the triathlon. The swimming part is simple, unless you are going to wear a wetsuit, in which case get your wetsuit fitted by a specialist swim or triathlon store. If you are swimming in open water you may need outdoor tinted goggles. Swim in your wetsuit to get used to how it affects your stroke and take your wetsuit off during training to make the transitions faster. Your bike needs to be set up correctly to enable you to be in a comfortable aerodynamic position and get the best power output. In training practice, get in and out of your cycling shoes quickly and try

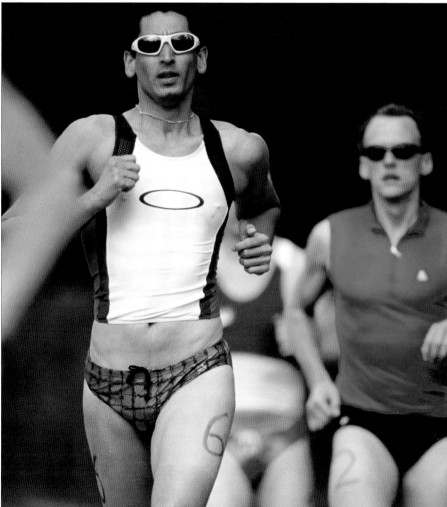

Left: When others are suffering in the later stages of the triathlon, a strong run will take you up the leader board rapidly.

Triathlon training plan

The following training plan assumes that you are training for an Olympic distance triathlon in about six weeks' time, that you have a good level of fitness and that you are able to train for six sessions per week, in addition to doing two strength/core sessions each week. Everyone responds differently to training sessions, so adjust your training to what suits you best. Practise your transition by doing a 'swim to bike' or 'bike to run', with no rest period. These are marked on the plan with a *.

	Monday	Tuesday	Wednesday	Thursday	Friday	Saturday	Sunday
Week 1	Swim 1	Cycle 1	Run 1	Swim 2	Rest	Cycle 4	Run 4
Week 2	Swim 4	Cycle 2	Run 2	Swim 3	Rest	Cycle 4	Run 4
Week 3	Swim 1	Cycle 1	Run 3	Swim 4	Rest	Cycle 3	Run 4
Week 4	Swim 3	Cycle 4	Run 3	*Swim 3 + Cycle 3	Cycle 1	Rest	*Cycle 1 + Run 1
Week 5	Swim 1	Cycle 1	Run 2	*Swim 4 + Cycle 2	Cycle 1	Rest	*Cycle 3 + Run 1
Week 6	Swim 4	Cycle 3	Run 30 mins L2	Swim 2	Rest	Cycle 40 mins L2	Race

Swim sessions

Warm up and cool down 100–200m/109–218yd, L1–L2

1 – timed 1,500m/1,640-yd swim, L3

2 – 10 x 100m/109-yd sprint at L3–L4 with 30 seconds' rest between each one

3 – 3 x 400m/437-yd at L3–L4 with 2 minutes' rest between each one

4 – 2 x 800m/875-yd at L3 with 4 minutes' rest between each one

Cycling sessions

Warm up and cool down for 5–10 minutes at L1–L2

1 – timed 20km/12.4-mile time trial on a flat route, L3–L4

2 – 6 x 4-minute hills at L4 with at least 5 minutes' rest between hills, L2

3 – 1½ hours with 20-second sprints every 5 minutes on flat route, L2–L3

4 – 2 hours using two gears too hard for the middle 10 minutes of every 30 minutes, L2–L3

Running sessions

Warm up and cool down with a 5-minute jog at L1–L2

1 – timed 10km/6-mile run on flat L3

2 – 8 x 2-minute runs on hills at L3–L4 with at least 4 minutes' easy jog between hills, L2

3 – 6 x 1,000m/1,094-yd fast L3–L4 on the flat with 500m/547-yd easy jog between them, L2

4 – 1 hour steady run, L2–L3

---

attaching them to the pedals before the start. Choose cycling shoes that are easy to get in and out of with minimum straps. For running, select shoes that are light and easy to get in and out of. Consider using elastic laces to save time.

Your weakest discipline

Every triathlete has a discipline that is not as strong as the other two. Spend time on your weakest discipline to bring it up to the standard of the others. Use the off-season to take advantage and double up on training sessions involving your weakest discipline. However, consider where you need to make the real improvements. If you are doing an Ironman and swimming is your weakest sport, you need a plan. Most of the time is spent on the bike and run so if you do shave off 5 minutes in the swim it will not make much difference to the outcome.

More time spent on the bike and running might mean that you can take a bigger chunk of time off the end result. In shorter sprint events it is more important to get each discipline to equal strength, and as fast as possible.

Training for triathlon is hard; listen to what your body tells you to avoid over-training and injuries. Rest is as important as your training. Practise swimming with others who are in training, especially in open water, to get used to having people surrounding you and get to know the conditions of open water. You may need to adjust your swimming stroke to have a higher arm action on recovery if the water conditions are rough.

Nutrition

Training for a triathlon will burn a massive number of calories, so you need to eat lots of low to medium GI foods every three to four hours to maintain energy levels, followed by medium to high GI foods in the two hours before, during and after training sessions so that you can replace muscle glycogen (stored glucose). Your body will be at risk of dehydration, so keep your fluid intake high and weigh yourself to test hydration levels after training sessions and competition.

Index

PICTURE ACKNOWLEDGEMENTS

The publisher would like to thank the following picture libraries for the use of their pictures in the book. Every effort has been made to acknowledge the pictures properly. We apologize if there are any unintentional omissions, which will be corrected in future editions.

l=left, r=right, t=top, b=bottom, c=centre

Alamy: 11bl, 14bl, 14br, 17bl, 43tr, 44b, 134, 135.
Corbis: 12 (both), 14t, 15bl, 18tr, 18bl, 42, 43b, 44t, 55bl, 60bl, 61tr, 61bc, 126br, 127, 138tl, 147, 150tr.
Getty: 9, 10tr, 10bl, 11, 13tl, 13b, 15cl, 15r, 16, 19bl, 19bc, 19br, 21br, 22 (both), 25cr, 25bl, 26 (all), 30, 31, 33tc, 33tr, 33b, 34t, 35b, 37tr, 38t, 40 (both), 41 (both), 54tl, 54tr, 54br, 55br, 58, 92, 93tl, 93tc, 93tr, 96br, 98bl, 120bl, 124 (both), 126bl, 129tr, 131tl, 132 (both), 133l, 136, 138bl, 140, 142tc, 142tr, 143bc, 143br, 144tr, 146bl, 148b, 149, 152tr, 152bl, 153tr, 155l, 155br, 156 (both).
iStockphoto: 43tl, 141.
Philip O'Connor: 6–7, 8, 10tl, 17t, 19t, 20 (both), 21tl, 21tr, 21bl, 23 (all), 24, 25tl, 25tr, 27 (both), 28 (both), 29 (all), 32, 34b, 35t, 36 (all), 37tl, 37b, 39 (all), 45, 46, 47 (all), 48 (both), 49, 50, 51 (all), 52, 53 (all), 54bl, 56 (all), 57 (all), 60cl, 62, 63 (all), 65 (all), 66–68, 69tl, 69tc, 69tr, 70tl, 70tr, 71 (all), 72tr, 72br, 73 (all), 74tr, 74br, 75 (all), 76cr, 77 (all), 78tr, 79 (all), 81 (all), 83 (all), 84br, 85 (all), 87 (all), 89 (all), 90bl, 91 (all), 94, 95, 98cr, 99 (all), 100–117, 120tr, 120br, 122tr, 137 (all), 138tr, 139 (both), 142bl, 142br, 145 (both), 146tr, 148tc, 148tr, 150bl, 152br, 155tr.
Photoshot: 18tl.
Science Photo Library: 80tl.